Productivity Smarts

Leaders and Managers Unlock Productivity Secrets from 12 Influential Muscicians of the 20th and 21st Century

Gerald J. Leonard

Copyright © 2025 by Gerald J. Leonard

All rights reserved.

No part of this book may be reproduced in any form or by any electronic or mechanical means, including information storage and retrieval systems, without written permission from the author, except for the use of brief quotations in a book review.

ISBN: 978-1-7340050-2-8

For Cloretta Stoudmire

Contents

Introduction — xi
The Productivity Parthenon — xv

Part One
Pillar One – Focus and Discipline
1. Prince — 5
2. Taylor Swift — 21
3. Beyoncé — 36

Part Two
Pillar Two – Reinvention and Innovation
4. David Bowie — 55
5. The Beatles — 71
6. Ed Sheeran — 86

Part Three
Pillar Three – Experimentation and Resilience
7. Frank Zappa — 103
8. Jimi Hendrix — 117
9. John Coltrane — 131

Part Four
Pillar Four – Collaboration and Vulnerability
10. Rihanna — 155
11. Justin Timberlake — 170
12. Billie Eilish — 182

Conclusion: Building Your Parthenon of Productivity   195
Acknowledgments   201

Praise for Gerald J. Leonard

"It's a must-read for anyone looking to elevate their creativity, leadership, and results to iconic levels." — **Patty Aubery,** President of The Canfield Training Group and Co-Creator of the Chicken Soup for the Soul Brand.

"Gerald Lenard has created something truly extraordinary with this book. By blending the magic of music with the mastery of productivity, he takes readers on an inspiring journey through the lives and leadership strategies of icons like The Beatles, Beyoncé, Taylor Swift, and Prince. This book doesn't just entertain—it offers profound insights into what it takes to achieve greatness in any field. It's a must-read for anyone looking to elevate their creativity, leadership, and results to iconic levels."

— **Patty Aubery**, President of The Canfield Training Group and Co-Creator of the *Chicken Soup for the Soul* Brand.

"Insightful, practical, and deeply inspiring—this book is a masterstroke in productivity and leadership. Gerald's passion for productivity and music is unprecedented. These combined with his insatiable appetite to keep on growing, learning and sharing his knowledge with leaders is very inspiring. If you are looking for the ultimate advantage in productivity, this is a must read."

— **Kenny Odetunde**, Master Platinum Results Coach, Business Results Trainer, Robbins Research International, Inc.

Unlocking Productivity Smarts: A Symphony of Success for Modern Leaders"
Imagine a playbook that combines the genius of legendary musi-

cians with actionable strategies to supercharge your productivity. *Productivity Smarts* does just that, weaving lessons from icons like Beyoncé, David Bowie, and Prince into a dynamic framework for managing teams, projects, and personal growth.

This book is built on **The Four Pillars of Productivity**— Focus, Innovation, Experimentation, and Collaboration—each inspired by music's greatest legends. From Prince's laser focus on mastering every detail to David Bowie's fearless reinvention, it's a masterclass in balancing creativity with discipline.

Key takeaways:

🎯 **Focus**: Channel your energy where it matters most, cutting through distractions like a pro.

Innovation: Stay relevant by embracing change and rethinking the status quo.

🎤 **Experimentation**: Take calculated risks and adapt to challenges with resilience.

Collaboration: Build harmony in teams through trust, vulnerability, and collective strength.

Whether you're leading a team or navigating personal goals, *Productivity Smarts* provides a roadmap to lasting success. Think of it as your backstage pass to productivity, inspired by the legends who turned their dreams into timeless masterpieces. 🎵

What's your productivity anthem? Let's build your Parthenon of success together! 🎤 #Leadership #Productivity #Innovation

Well worth a read

— **Dr. Allen Steven Lycka** | The FAMOUS Dr. AL | The Doctor of Positivity & Happiness, 3X Best Selling Author | Keynote, TEDx Speaker | Syndicated Radio Show Host , www.DrAl.Live

"A revolutionary book that merges music and leadership insights into actionable tools for productivity. Gerald's work will inspire you to think differently about success."

— **Reshma Sheikh**, MSDUK - Managing Director / CEO Whisperer / NED / Consultant / Public Speaker

"Gerald's unique perspective on productivity is a game-changer. This book will inspire leaders and managers alike. I love the tie-in to music and musicians."
   — **John Kremer**, The Book Marketing Ambassador of Fun, Author of 1001 Ways to Market Your Books

"Iconic and transformational leaders in the field of music have left a legacy of gifts for anyone seeking greater innovation and productivity. Gerald Leonard's rich experience in both music and business has built a bridge for us to receive those gifts. Open the book and you will open creative insights and fresh inspiration to empower your business leadership and success."
   — **Paul R. Scheele, PhD**, CEO, Scheele Learning Systems, Co-founder and Chairman of Learning Strategies Corporation

"Productivity Smarts is an essential read for leaders looking to learn innovative strategies from the world of music."
   —**Joe Rose,** Co-Founder, Turnberry Solutions, Inc.

"Gerald's deep passion for music, and ambition for business execution is on full display in Productivity Smarts. I've never seen another author creatively combined these two concepts into a strategy for success in business and leadership!"
   — **Sheldon Barrocks**, Author of Unstuck Mondays: A Guide to Growing in Your Creativity and Career

"Gerald is one of those unique individuals who has been able to combine two of his life passions - productivity and music!
   Having spent decades perfecting the knowledge that has led him to be an expert in both, he has surpassed past books by digging deep into their intricacies and come up with a book that again shows that success isn't simply a product of raw talent or hard work alone—it's the outcome of discipline, structure, focus, and the ability to consistently not only deliver results

under pressure but also continually work on the improvements."

—**Jean S Chawapiwa**, Head of Member Services MSDUK

Introduction

In the worlds of both music and business, success isn't simply a product of raw talent or hard work alone—it's the outcome of discipline, structure, focus, and the ability to consistently deliver results under pressure. Over the years, I've spent countless hours as both a professional musician and a business leader, and I've discovered a profound connection between these two seemingly different arenas. The principles that drive productivity in music, when applied correctly, can be equally powerful for those navigating the challenges of managing teams, projects, and portfolios in the business world.

This book, *Productivity Smarts: What Managers and Leaders Can Learn about the Productivity Secrets from 12 Iconic Musicians of the 20th and 21st Centuries*, is designed to help managers and leaders tap into the universal truths of productivity—truths that have been perfected by musicians at the top of their game, but that translate seamlessly into the high-stakes, high-pressure environment of modern business. The goal of this book is not only to share insights but to provide you with concrete strategies you can implement right away to improve the way you and your team work.

Introduction

Why This Book and Why Now?

The modern business environment is more complex than ever. Managers and leaders are asked to juggle an increasing number of responsibilities, oversee multiple projects, and balance short-term goals with long-term strategic vision. Thriving in this kind of environment requires more than traditional time-management techniques—it calls for a new way of thinking about productivity itself.

At its core, *Productivity Smarts* is a guide for professionals who are looking for something more than quick-fix solutions. It's for people who want to build lasting productivity habits that not only help them get through today's challenges but also position them for long-term success. Whether you're leading a large team, overseeing an important project, or simply trying to better manage your own time and energy, this book is designed to help you rethink your approach.

In each chapter, we'll explore a legendary musician's superpower—integral to musical success—that can help you unlock your team's productivity. But it's not just about abstract concepts. The goal here is to provide you with actionable insights you can immediately apply. By the end of this book, you'll have a comprehensive toolkit of strategies that can be tailored to your specific work environment, helping you and your team perform at a higher level.

How to Use This Book

One of the most important things I want you to take away from this book is that productivity is not a one-size-fits-all solution. What works for one person or one organization may not work for another. That's why *Productivity Smarts* is designed to be flexible and adaptable. It's not about rigid systems or restrictive processes. Instead, it's about understanding the underlying principles of productivity so that you can apply them in a way that makes sense for your unique situation.

Think of this book as a roadmap. Each chapter introduces a new concept—one that has been drawn from the world of music but is

Introduction

equally relevant in business. For example, we'll talk about how the discipline of staying focused, so critical to a musician's success, can be translated into your daily work routines. We'll dive deep into the concept of collaboration, examining how musicians work together to create harmony—and how you can foster a similar sense of teamwork and cohesion within your organization.

As you read through the chapters, I encourage you to think about how these concepts apply to your own experience. You may find that some ideas resonate more with you than others—and that's okay. The goal is not to follow every recommendation to the letter but to pick and choose the strategies that make the most sense for you and your team. Productivity is personal, and this book is designed to empower you to make informed decisions about how to improve it.

Each chapter also includes practical exercises and reflection prompts to help you put these concepts into practice. Whether it's refining your daily routines, improving communication within your team, or developing more effective ways to manage your workload, these exercises are designed to move you from theory to action. The goal is to create lasting change—not just temporary boosts in productivity.

A Fresh Approach to Productivity

What sets *Productivity Smarts* apart from other productivity books is its focus on the creative process. Too often, productivity is seen as a mechanical process—something that can be optimized and systematized like an assembly line. However, creativity and innovation, which are critical in both music and business, don't work that way. They require flexibility, spontaneity, and room for experimentation.

Throughout this book, we'll explore how you can strike a balance between structure and creativity in your work. Just as musicians create masterpieces through a combination of disciplined practice and improvisation, you can create a productive work environment by fostering both focus and flexibility. It's about finding the right rhythm

Introduction

—one that allows you to stay on track while also being open to new ideas and approaches.

In the business world, projects rarely go exactly as planned. Deadlines shift, priorities change, and unforeseen challenges arise. That's why it's so important to build a productivity system that is both strong and adaptable—one that can withstand the pressures of the modern business environment without breaking. This is where the lessons from music can be so valuable. Musicians know how to stay focused and deliver results, even when the conditions aren't perfect. They know how to adapt without losing sight of the end goal. And they know how to work together to create something greater than the sum of its parts.

Moving Forward

As we move through this book, I encourage you to keep an open mind. Some of the ideas may challenge your current approach to productivity, while others may feel immediately familiar. The key is to approach this journey with a sense of curiosity and a willingness to experiment. Productivity, like music, is an evolving process. What works today may need to be adjusted tomorrow, and that's okay. The goal is not perfection—it's progress.

By the end of this book, I hope you will have not only a deeper understanding of productivity but also a renewed sense of energy and enthusiasm for your work. The strategies you'll learn are designed to help you and your team perform at your best, not just in the short term but for the long haul. Whether you're managing a large portfolio of projects, leading a small team, or striving to improve your personal workflow, *Productivity Smarts* will give you the tools and insights you need to succeed.

So let's get started. Together, we'll explore how the lessons from the world of music can transform the way you approach productivity—both for yourself and for your team. Let's find your rhythm and unlock the full potential of your work.

The Productivity Parthenon

The Parthenon, perched high above Athens, stands as a timeless testament to balance, beauty, and resilience. More than just a temple dedicated to Athena, it represents an achievement of harmony between form and function. Its architects were not merely builders but visionaries who created something enduring, inspiring, and purposeful. Every element of its design, from the curvature of its columns to the optical illusions that make it appear flawless, was deliberate, demonstrating how intentionality and precision can produce greatness.

In many ways, the Parthenon serves as a metaphor for modern workplaces. Just as its creators balanced structural strength with aesthetic elegance, organizations today must harmonize productivity with creativity, efficiency with innovation, and individual effort with collaboration. The principles that shaped this iconic structure centuries ago remain profoundly relevant to managing portfolios, leading teams, and executing projects in a world that constantly demands more. The Parthenon reminds us that enduring success, whether in architecture or business, results from thoughtful design, deliberate choices, and an unwavering commitment to purpose.

Its architects faced a complex challenge: constructing a space that was both functional and symbolic. As a sacred place for worship, the Parthenon had to fulfill its immediate purpose, yet it also stood as a representation of Athena's wisdom and the glory of Athens. Similarly, modern organizations must balance the practical needs of day-to-day operations with the broader vision of their goals. Processes, roles, and workflows must align not only to achieve short-term success but also to build something lasting and meaningful. The Parthenon's columns, each unique yet interdependent, are a powerful symbol of this balance—distinct elements that, together, create an unshakeable foundation.

This interdependence forms the basis of what we call the Four Pillars of Productivity. Just as the Parthenon relies on its columns for strength and stability, productivity in the workplace depends on focus, innovation, experimentation, and collaboration. These pillars are not just abstract ideals; they are actionable principles that underpin success in any field. Focus and discipline form the foundation, much like the precise mathematical principles that guided the Parthenon's construction. Reinvention and innovation ensure relevance and adaptability, reflecting how the Parthenon was built upon the remains of its predecessor, repurposing materials to create something even greater. Experimentation and resilience enable growth and sustainability, mirroring the Parthenon's ability to withstand centuries of natural and human challenges. Collaboration and vulnerability, the final pillar, reflects the collective effort of the architects, laborers, and artisans who brought the Parthenon to life. It reminds us that success is rarely achieved alone.

These pillars also resonate deeply with the practices of legendary music icons who, in their own ways, are modern-day architects of excellence. Prince exemplified focus and discipline, meticulously controlling every aspect of his music and performances to achieve perfection. David Bowie mastered reinvention, continually evolving to stay ahead of his time and inspiring others to adapt and innovate.

Beyoncé has demonstrated an unparalleled work ethic and a relentless pursuit of excellence that ensures every detail of her craft is executed flawlessly. Ed Sheeran epitomizes the value of consistent output, producing an astonishing number of songs through structured creativity. Each of these artists, like the builders of the Parthenon, achieved greatness by balancing structure and creativity, discipline and innovation.

The Parthenon's legacy is not just in its design but in the lessons it offers for constructing success in any endeavor. Focus and discipline enable us to prioritize and execute our goals with precision. Reinvention and innovation challenge us to push boundaries and embrace change. Experimentation and resilience encourage us to take calculated risks, learn from failures, and adapt to challenges. Collaboration and vulnerability teach us to build trust, communicate openly, and leverage the strengths of others to achieve something greater than ourselves. These principles are as relevant to managing a business as they are to creating a timeless masterpiece.

Workplaces, like orchestras, thrive on harmony. Each role, like an instrument, contributes something unique, yet success depends on alignment and unity. The Parthenon's columns symbolize this interconnectedness, standing strong only because of their collective support. Similarly, the music icons featured in this book demonstrate how individual strengths, when aligned with broader goals, create extraordinary results. Their lives and careers offer a powerful lens through which to explore the Four Pillars of Productivity, providing practical insights for achieving success in modern workplaces.

As you delve into the stories of these artists, you'll uncover strategies for leading teams, managing resources, and fostering creativity in your projects. From Prince's laser-sharp focus to Bowie's transformative reinvention, from Beyoncé's tireless work ethic to Billie Eilish's emotional vulnerability, their practices offer lessons that transcend music, becoming blueprints for productivity in any field.

The Parthenon teaches us that greatness comes from balance. Its architects achieved harmony between form and function, tradition and innovation, individuality and teamwork. By embracing these principles, you can build your own Parthenon of productivity—a workplace that is not only efficient but inspiring, not only successful but enduring. Like the Parthenon, your masterpiece will stand the test of time. Let's begin.

Athena, the goddess of wisdom, strategy, and discipline, was the inspiration behind the Parthenon. Revered not only for her intellect but also for her strategic acumen, Athena represents the perfect balance of thought and action. In Greek mythology, she was a guiding force for heroes and leaders alike, offering clarity in times of uncertainty and strength in moments of challenge. Her presence atop the Acropolis was a constant reminder to the Athenians of the power of foresight, planning, and execution.

In the modern world, Athena's principles are just as vital. Productivity mastery begins with strategy—having the wisdom to see the bigger picture and the discipline to break it into achievable steps. Athena's influence isn't just about intelligence; it's about applying that intelligence in a structured way to achieve meaningful outcomes. Her wisdom teaches us that success is rarely accidental. Instead, it's the result of careful planning, clear priorities, and consistent effort.

Imagine Athena standing beside you as you face the complexities of the modern workplace. Her shield reflects your goals, protecting you from distractions, while her spear symbolizes the precision needed to execute tasks effectively. Athena doesn't simply command victory; she prepares for it. Her approach is deliberate, thoughtful, and methodical—exactly the qualities required to master productivity.

Setting the stage for productivity mastery starts with clarity. Athena's strategic wisdom reminds us to define what success looks like. This begins with asking critical questions: What are your ultimate objectives? How do your daily tasks align with those goals? Are your efforts focused on what truly matters? Too often, individuals and teams lose themselves in busyness, mistaking activity for progress. Athena's discipline serves as a reminder to focus on priorities, ensuring every action contributes to the overarching strategy.

Discipline is the second piece of Athena's legacy. Wisdom alone isn't enough to achieve greatness; it must be paired with the consistent effort to bring plans to life. Discipline means staying the course even when distractions threaten to pull you away. It's the ability to set boundaries, maintain momentum, and resist the temptation of immediate gratification in favor of long-term success. In the same way that the Parthenon's architects adhered to precise measurements and principles, Athena's discipline ensures that your efforts remain aligned and purposeful.

Athena also embodies resilience. She understands that challenges are inevitable and that strategy must adapt to unforeseen circumstances. Just as she guided heroes through battles with clever tactics, she reminds us that productivity isn't about perfection—it's about persistence. Productivity mastery doesn't mean avoiding mistakes; it means learning from them, refining your approach, and continuing forward with renewed determination.

In the workplace, embracing Athena's qualities means setting the stage for sustained success. Start with a clear vision, then develop a strategy to achieve it. Break it down into actionable steps, assign responsibilities, and establish timelines. But don't stop there. Adopt a mindset of continuous improvement, regularly evaluating your progress and adjusting your strategy as needed. Above all, maintain the discipline to stay focused, ensuring that every effort aligns with your ultimate objectives.

As we explore the Four Pillars of Productivity in this book, Athena's influence will remain a guiding force. Her wisdom will inspire focus and discipline, her strategic vision will encourage reinvention and innovation, and her resilience will reinforce the importance of experimentation. Like the Parthenon that was built in her honor, Athena's principles offer a timeless blueprint for success, whether you're managing a project, leading a team, or navigating the complexities of modern life. Her legacy is a call to action: think deeply, plan wisely, and act with purpose. With Athena as your guide, the stage is set for mastering productivity and achieving greatness.

Part One

Pillar One – Focus and Discipline

The Foundation of Excellence

In the symphony of productivity, focus and discipline form the bedrock upon which all other achievements rest. These two qualities are the pillars that allow creativity to flourish, innovation to take shape, and collaboration to succeed. Without focus, even the most ambitious ideas can scatter into fragments. Without discipline, the best-laid plans falter under the weight of inconsistency. Together, they are the force that transforms potential into accomplishment.

Focus is the art of knowing where to direct your energy, about how to align every effort with a clear goal. It's the lens that sharpens your vision, filtering out distractions and keeping you anchored to what truly matters. Discipline, on the other hand, is the steady rhythm that sustains momentum. It's the commitment to show up, to work through challenges, and to deliver results even when motivation wavers. When these qualities merge, they create a powerful engine for excellence, one that propels individuals and teams toward their objectives with unwavering precision.

Few artists embody these traits more profoundly than Prince, Taylor Swift, and Beyoncé. Each of these legends mastered focus and discipline in their own unique way, demonstrating how these principles can be applied to any craft or profession. Prince's meticulous attention to detail, Taylor Swift's goal-oriented mindset, and Beyoncé's relentless work ethic provide us with a blueprint for achieving greatness.

Prince was a master of control. From songwriting and producing to performing and even designing his album covers, he was deeply involved in every aspect of his work. His ability to focus on the minutiae of his craft without losing sight of the bigger picture allowed him to create music that remains timeless. For Prince, focus wasn't just about eliminating distractions; it was about channeling his energy into perfecting every detail. His discipline ensured that no part of his process was left to chance, resulting in work that reflected his singular vision.

Taylor Swift, by contrast, offers a lesson in strategic focus. Her career is a masterclass in balancing creativity with business acumen. From meticulously planning album releases to navigating the ever-changing music industry, Swift exemplifies the power of setting long-term goals while managing the day-to-day demands of her craft. Her ability to stay focused on her vision while adapting to new challenges demonstrates how discipline can amplify creativity, ensuring that artistic expression is aligned with strategic objectives.

Then there's Beyoncé, whose unparalleled work ethic sets a gold standard for preparation and execution. Her performances are known for their precision and intensity, but what often goes unseen is the rigorous preparation that makes them possible. Hours of rehearsals, relentless attention to detail, and a commitment to perfection define her process. Beyoncé's discipline is not just about working hard—it's about working smart and planning every element of her craft to ensure excellence at every level.

The lessons from these icons are clear. Focus and discipline are not about perfection—they're about intentionality. They're about defining your goals with clarity, aligning your actions with those goals, and committing to the process with persistence. Whether you're leading a project, managing a team, or pursuing a personal ambition, these qualities are essential for turning vision into reality.

In the chapters ahead, we'll delve deeper into how Prince, Taylor Swift, and Beyoncé harnessed focus and discipline to achieve extraordinary results. More importantly, we'll explore how you can apply their practices to your own work. From setting priorities and managing time to maintaining momentum and refining your craft, this pillar will equip you with the tools to excel in any endeavor.

Focus and discipline may not always be glamorous, but they are the quiet forces behind every great achievement. As you step into this pillar, consider how these principles can sharpen your vision, strengthen your resolve, and set the stage for your own masterpiece.

Chapter 1
Prince

"I don't need any pyro; I am the special effects." —Prince

Prince's Essential iTunes Playlist:

In the tapestry of music legends, Prince stands as a vivid thread, weaving a narrative of extraordinary focus and discipline. This chapter explores the less visible yet profoundly impactful elements of

Prince's life—his unwavering dedication and meticulous approach to his craft.

Born in 1958 into a world filled with music, Prince Rogers Nelson showed signs of his future greatness from a young age. His father, a jazz pianist, and his mother, a singer, laid the foundation. Young Prince was not merely a passive recipient of these influences; he absorbed them with an intense focus that belied his years.

His early life wasn't without its challenges. His parents divorced when he was young. He was small, quiet, and "different," and thus was subject to teasing and bullying. Prince's passion for music and dedication to his craft helped him rise above his circumstances.

- **A Childhood of Discipline:** Even during his childhood, Prince's life was marked by a rigorous discipline with music. Hours spent in practice were not a chore but a chosen pursuit, a clear indication of his deep passion and focus.

As Prince stepped into the world of professional music, his discipline became even more pronounced. He wasn't just playing music; he was living it. His early albums, especially *For You*, were testaments to his dedication. He played 27 instruments, a feat that showcased not just talent but a disciplined approach to learning and mastering multiple skills.

- **Unwavering Focus:** His relentless focus was evident in the studio, where he was known to work for days without a break, perfecting every beat, every note. This level of dedication was rare, even in the demanding world of music.

Prince was a prolific songwriter known for his innovative approach to music. Albums like *Purple Rain* (1984) and *Sign o' the Times* (1987) feature a blend of genres, from funk and R&B to rock

Productivity Smarts

and pop. His ability to write, produce, and perform music across genres demonstrates his disciplined approach to creativity and his focus on innovation.

Prince maintained strict control over his music and image. He was involved in every aspect of his work, from composing and producing to arranging and performing. This control extended to his interactions with record labels. He famously battled Warner Bros. for creative freedom, which led to him changing his name to an unpronounceable symbol.

Throughout his career, Prince continually evolved his musical style and image. He was not afraid to experiment with new sounds, as evidenced in albums like *Lovesexy* (1988) and *The Gold Experience* (1995). This constant reinvention required a disciplined approach to learning and a focused exploration of new artistic directions.

In 1987, Prince built Paisley Park, his private estate and production complex. This venture required immense focus and discipline, not only in its conception and construction but also in its use as a creative space where he could work without constraints.

The Minneapolis Sound, synonymous with Prince, wasn't just a genre—it was a revolution. Crafting this unique sound required more than just creativity; it required a laser-focused approach to fuse rock, funk, pop, and R&B into a seamless, infectious rhythm. This sound was a cornerstone of albums like *1999* (1982). His focus on developing this distinct style played a significant role in shaping the music of the 1980s.

- **Discipline in Innovation:** Creating and perfecting this sound demanded a disciplined experimentation with different styles and instruments. Prince's studio, Paisley Park, became a laboratory for this musical alchemy.

Prince's live performances were electrifying, a whirlwind of energy and charisma. His rigorous touring schedules, including the famous "Purple Rain" tour, required a high level of discipline and stamina. His ability to deliver consistently high-energy and engaging performances speaks to his focus and dedication.

- **Mastery of the Stage:** His discipline extended to his physical fitness and vocal training, ensuring that every performance was not just a show but an embodiment of his musical vision.

Prince's untimely passing in 2016 at age 57 left a void in the world of music, but his legacy of focus and discipline continues to inspire. His life was a testament to the power of dedication in honing one's craft. Prince's work ethic was legendary. He was known for his prolific output, often releasing more than one album a year, and he left behind a vast vault of unreleased material. This productivity was a result of his disciplined routine and focused approach to music-making.

- **Inspiration for Generations:** Emerging artists often look to Prince not just for his musical genius but for his approach to life and art. His discipline, coupled with his focus, made him an icon, transcending the boundaries of genre and time.

In a world where distractions are plenty, Prince's life serves as a beacon, guiding aspiring artists and professionals alike toward the harmony of disciplined pursuit.

As the notes of his music continue to resonate, Prince's legacy in the realms of focus and discipline stands as a powerful reminder of what passion, when coupled with hard work, can achieve—a symphony that continues to inspire long after the final note has faded.

In my journey toward mastering the bass, I encountered a pivotal moment in college that reshaped my understanding of what discipline and focus meant. There exists an intricate relationship between these two superpowers, which is obvious in the narrative about the legendary artist Prince. These same superpowers are also needed in Project Management, from setting goals to creating a strategic plan and, more importantly, executing that plan.

In my teens, I learned to play electric bass, and I was oblivious to the classical realm. It wasn't until college that I ventured into the world of upright, double bass playing, a late start by conventional standards. I realized I wanted to pursue music as a career, but I needed to learn to play music on an instrument I wasn't as familiar with using techniques I hadn't known about, let alone master. I was exchanging a guitar pick for a bow. Many of my peers were already advanced, preparing for prestigious institutions like Juilliard or the Cincinnati Conservatory. However, my path was different.

I had played a little double bass in high school bands and had a basic foundation, but college was where I truly immersed myself in serious study. But I had a rocky start. Because there was a lack of an orchestra and a bass teacher at my historically black college, I had to be resourceful. I learned bowing from a violinist and scales from etude books, spending hours in the practice room after classes. Not exactly the easiest or most efficient way to master an instrument, but I was focused and determined to learn.

After classes, I spent four to five hours in the practice room, running scales and playing etudes until my hands hurt. I didn't watch television and had a minimal social life. Learning to master the bass was my vision. I would be at the music building when it opened and played in the evening until it was time to kick me out.

This self-taught journey was arduous but rewarding. My dedication saw me growing rapidly in skill, leading to an audition and subsequent acceptance into the Springfield Symphony in Ohio. This achievement was significant, given my unconventional training background. This was a professional orchestra in which I got paid. We had only about eight concerts a year, so the money was by no means making me rich, but it did provide enough income to get a car, one big enough for my enormous instrument so that I had my own ride to rehearsals and concerts.

Playing in a professional orchestra as a college student was an unparalleled experience. I listened to the works of Beethoven, Stravinsky, and Brahms or whatever piece we were performing. I had the sheet music and would play along with the music with my double bass. By the time I went to rehearsals, I was familiar with the music. This self-imposed discipline was crucial in a setting where formal orchestral training was absent.

My growth soon outpaced my teacher's ability to guide me. He was a violin player and teacher, not double bass. In order to improve and meet the demands of the orchestra, I needed someone who taught bass specifically. He recommended that I work with Debbie Wright, a seasoned musician with ties to several prestigious orchestras. Under her tutelage, I expanded my repertoire, embracing both jazz and classical styles. I grew in my abilities. My schedule was packed with school, lessons, symphony, and practice. I was more motivated than ever to improve, and my eye never went off the prize.

Debbie told me about Barry Green, who was the principal of the Cincinnati Symphony. She suggested I start taking lessons with him. At the same time, I learned about a guy named Frank Proto, who was also a bassist for the Cincinnati Symphony. He was different than Barry, who focused mostly on classical technique. Frank was a classical and jazz bassist. In addition, he was a composer and wrote jingles. I was still living near the campus of Central State University in Wilberforce, Ohio, and it would require moving to make it work.

I learned that Frank wrote music for a gentleman named Francois Rabbath, who had lived in Paris but was in the States and performed a lot of Frank's works. When Frank came to Springfield to play a recital, I was there. He had a tight ensemble consisting of a violin, a violist, and him. One of the pieces they performed started like a typical classical string trio piece, but then, in the middle, the violin and violist put down their bows and started plucking jazz chords and rhythm. Frank began playing a jazz solo on his bass.

At that moment, I thought, *That's it. That's what I want to do. Classical and jazz!*

After the recital, I introduced myself.

"I'd like to study with you."

"I appreciate you thinking of me, but I don't teach a lot of students. Right now, I have two."

This is where the focus came in. I knew what I wanted and wasn't willing to give up so easily.

"Would you reconsider when you have an opening?"

He could tell I wasn't going to let it go so easily.

"You realize I am in Cincinnati, right?" he countered.

This was around 75 miles away from Springfield. Again, this wasn't going to stop me.

"I'm thinking of applying to school at the University of Cincinnati," I blurted out. I was weighing my options for grad school but hadn't really seriously considered it until that moment.

"Have you considered Barry Green? Most bassists that come to Cincinnati become his students. He has a much larger teaching studio than me."

"I had considered Barry, but after hearing you...you were amazing. I want to learn classical and jazz, and I love your sound technique."

He finally relented. "If you make it into the conservatory, here is my number. We can talk further then."

I didn't wait. I called him all the time. I was again focused on my goal—to become Frank Proto's student. I did get into the University of Cincinnati University, and they gave me a full scholarship.

Reflecting on my journey, the parallels with Prince's storied career become evident. His discipline and focus on music, much like my own experiences, highlight the importance of these virtues in achieving excellence. Whether it's mastering an instrument or tackling a complex project, discipline and focus play a crucial role in orchestrating success.

This narrative, though rooted in music, transcends its boundaries.

It's a testament to the power of focus and discipline in any field of endeavor. As you navigate your projects, remember the lessons from these musical journeys. Like a well-composed symphony, let discipline and focus guide your path to productivity and success.

> *"The greatest glory in living lies not in never falling, but in rising every time we fall."* —Nelson Mandela

Prince's productivity superpower, intense focus, and discipline are crucial for professionals. In the corporate world, maintaining concentration on tasks and being disciplined in work habits is essential for achieving goals and delivering results. Prince's ability to immerse himself in his craft for extended periods demonstrates the value of sustained effort and dedication in a world often filled with distractions. Adopting a similar approach can enhance productivity and lead to meaningful accomplishments in the professional realm.

Psychology:
Emotional Intelligence (EI) Impact on Leadership: Leaders with high emotional intelligence tend to have more successful teams. A study by the Consortium for Research on Emotional Intelligence in Organizations found that leaders with high EI outperform their counterparts in leadership effectiveness.

Neuroscience:
The Impact of Stress on Decision-Making: Chronic stress can impair decision-making processes. Research published in the journal *Nature* suggests that stress alters neural pathways, particularly in areas related to decision-making and emotional regulation.

Productivity Smarts

Business:
Employee Engagement and Productivity: Engaged employees are more productive and contribute to a positive work culture. Gallup's "State of the Global Workplace" report indicates that only 15% of employees worldwide are engaged in their jobs, emphasizing the potential for improvement in workplace engagement.

These interdisciplinary insights highlight the interconnected nature of psychology, neuroscience, and business, providing valuable perspectives for understanding human behavior, decision-making processes, and organizational dynamics.

- "The only limit to our realization of tomorrow will be our doubts of today." —Franklin D. Roosevelt

- "The greatest glory in living lies not in never falling, but in rising every time we fall." —Nelson Mandela

- "The only way to do great work is to love what you do." — Steve Jobs

Here are some thought-provoking questions that you should consider:

What are my core values, and am I living in alignment with them?

Am I in a position that allows me to utilize my strengths and skills effectively?

How do I contribute positively to the lives of those around me?

Do I surround myself with people who inspire and uplift me?

In what ways am I challenging myself to grow and learn?

What habits or beliefs might be holding me back from reaching my full potential?

What habits contribute to my overall health, and are there areas for improvement?

What legacy do I want to leave behind?

Productivity Smarts

These questions can serve as starting points for self-reflection and personal growth, encouraging you to explore various aspects of your life and make intentional choices for a more fulfilling and purpose-driven existence as you reflect on what you've learned about Prince.

Prince's Versatility: Prince's ability to play 27 instruments on his debut album is analogous to a project manager's need to understand various aspects of a project. This level of expertise ensures that a project manager can effectively oversee and integrate diverse project elements.

- **Lesson:** Develop a broad skill set and deep understanding of your project's components to manage effectively.

Blending Genres: Just as Prince blended genres in albums like *Purple Rain*, a project manager should be adept at integrating different methodologies and approaches to achieve project goals.

- **Lesson:** Embrace innovative approaches in project planning and execution for unique and effective solutions.

Control over Work: Prince's firm control over his music and image reflects the importance of strong leadership in project management. It's crucial to guide a project's vision and ensure alignment with goals.

- **Lesson:** Maintain clear leadership and direction to steer your project toward its intended outcome.

Developing a Signature Style: Prince's creation of the "Minneapolis Sound" illustrates the importance of developing a unique project identity or brand, which can help stand out and gain recognition.

- **Lesson:** Foster a unique identity for your projects to enhance visibility and impact.

Consistent Live Performances: Prince's exemplary performances mirror the need for consistently high-quality execution in project management. This involves ensuring that every phase of the project is executed to the best possible standard.

- **Lesson:** Strive for excellence in execution to ensure project success and stakeholder satisfaction.

Constantly Evolving: Prince's continual evolution is a lesson in keeping projects relevant and adaptive in changing environments.

- **Lesson:** Regularly reassess and adapt your project strategies to stay ahead of the curve.

Productivity Smarts

Creating a Dedicated Space: Prince's creation of Paisley Park serves as an example of turning a vision into reality, akin to taking a project from conception to completion.

- **Lesson:** Meticulously plan and execute your project vision, ensuring every detail aligns with the end goal.

Exceptional Productivity: Prince's legendary work ethic and prolific output highlight the importance of discipline and focus in managing projects effectively.

- **Lesson:** Cultivate a disciplined approach and maintain focus to ensure consistent productivity in your projects.

Prince's career offers profound lessons in managing projects with discipline, innovation, and focus. By emulating these qualities, project managers can orchestrate successful outcomes, much like Prince created timeless music.

As you manage your projects, ask yourself: Are you as versatile and knowledgeable about your project's various elements? Are you leading with clarity and vision? Are you open to innovative solutions and adapting to change? Reflecting on these questions and applying the "Prince" approach can elevate your project management skills to new heights.

Step 1: Self-Assessment
Begin by assessing your current time management habits. Reflect on how you currently allocate your time throughout the day and identify any patterns or habits that may be hindering your focus and productivity.

Step 2: Prioritize Goals
Identify your short-term and long-term goals. What are the most important tasks that will contribute significantly to these goals? Prioritize them based on their impact on your overall objectives.

Step 3: Time Audit
For a week, keep a detailed record of where you focus your attention and how you spend your time. Note every activity, no matter how small. This will give you a clear picture of where your focus and time is going and help identify areas for improvement.

Step 4: Identify Time Wasters
Review your time audit and identify activities that are not contributing to your goals. These might be time wasters or unnecessary tasks that can be minimized or eliminated.

Step 5: Set SMART Goals
Based on your priorities, set Specific, Measurable, Achievable, Relevant, and Time-bound (SMART) goals. Break these goals down into smaller, actionable tasks.

Step 6: Create a Schedule
Develop a daily or weekly schedule that aligns with your goals

and priorities. Allocate specific time blocks for different tasks, ensuring that high-priority activities are given adequate attention.

Step 7: Implement Time Blocking
Use the technique of time blocking, where you dedicate specific blocks of time to particular types of activities. This helps minimize multitasking and increases focus on the task at hand.

Step 8: Learn to Say No
Practice saying no to tasks or commitments that do not align with your goals. This helps you avoid overcommitting and ensures that your time is spent on activities that truly matter.

Step 9: Use Time Management Tools
Explore and adopt time management tools, such as calendars, to-do lists, or productivity apps. These tools can help you stay organized and on track with your schedule.

Step 10: Regularly Review and Adjust
Regularly review your time management strategies. Are you achieving your goals? Are there adjustments needed in your schedule? Be flexible and willing to make changes based on what works best for you.

Step 11: Celebrate Progress
Acknowledge and celebrate your successes along the way. Recognizing your achievements, no matter how small, can help reinforce positive time management habits.

Step 12: Seek Feedback
Ask for feedback from colleagues, friends, or mentors. They may offer valuable insights and suggestions for further improvement.

Remember, improvement takes time, and each person's journey is unique. Consistency and a willingness to adapt are key factors in enhancing your focus, discipline, and time management skills.

Take your productivity to the next level with cutting-edge neuroscience insights delivered straight to your inbox—join now:

Chapter 2
Taylor Swift

Her productivity superpower is her ability to focus on her goals and work tirelessly to achieve them.

"I think about my next move ten steps ahead of where I'm standing. I visualize where I want to be and take calculated steps to get there. I work hard to keep moving toward my goals, no matter what."
—Taylor Swift

Taylor Swift's Essential iTunes Playlist:

Gerald J. Leonard

. . .

In the vast tapestry of the music industry, the story of Taylor Swift stands as a radiant thread woven with ambition, resilience, and an unwavering commitment to authenticity. Born in Reading, Pennsylvania, Taylor emerged into a world where melodies resonated in her soul. Her parents, a stockbroker father and a mother immersed in mutual fund marketing, recognized the spark in their daughter and nurtured her burgeoning talent.

From local stages to the heart of country music in Nashville, Taylor's journey began at a tender age. The family's decision to relocate when Taylor was 14 was a pivotal moment, indicative of a family's belief in the extraordinary potential of their daughter. However, the Nashville scene, though fertile ground for musical dreams, posed challenges. Taylor faced skepticism about her youth and perceived lack of experience, yet these hurdles became the stepping stones to her remarkable ascent.

In the crucible of criticism, Taylor found her voice. Armed with a pen and a determination to prove her detractors wrong, she transformed setbacks into fuel for her artistic fire. The narrative shifted when she had a profound realization—a pivotal "aha" moment. Taylor understood that conforming to the expectations of a traditional country singer was stifling her true potential. Embracing her uniqueness became the catalyst for a seismic shift in her music, ushering in a genre-defying style that transcended conventional boundaries.

This metamorphosis marked the beginning of Taylor's ascent to stardom. Her journey, once characterized by the struggle of a young musician navigating Nashville's competitive terrain, evolved into a global phenomenon. Taylor Swift, now a chart-topping pop sensation, graced stages worldwide, collecting accolades and filling stadiums with devoted fans.

At the core of Taylor's prodigious success lies a productivity superpower—her unparalleled focus on goals. Tirelessly dedicated to her craft, she immersed herself in the art of songwriting, spent exhaustive hours in the recording studio, perfected her performances through rigorous rehearsals, and pioneered innovative marketing strategies. Her commitment to excellence was the cornerstone of a career marked by staggering statistics—over 100 million albums sold globally, 14 Grammy Awards, and a net worth surpassing $1 billion.

In the pages of *Time* magazine, Taylor was recognized as one of the world's most influential people, solidifying her status as a cultural icon. Yet, beyond the numbers and accolades, Taylor's beliefs form the beating heart of her journey. Rooted in hard work, perseverance, and authenticity, her philosophy is encapsulated in a simple yet profound mantra: "The lesson I've learned the most often in life is that you're always going to know more in the future than you know now."

Influenced by musical luminaries like Shania Twain, Dolly Parton, and the Dixie Chicks, Taylor drew inspiration from their ability to tell compelling stories through music. Their influence shaped her artistic vision, fostering a deep connection with her audience.

The saga of Taylor Swift is an epic tale of determination and evolution. From the intimate stages of local performances to the grandeur of global stardom, Taylor's journey encapsulates the spirit of a tireless artist committed to growth and authenticity. Her productivity superpower, manifested in an unwavering focus on goals, serves as a guiding light for aspiring musicians and professionals alike. Taylor Swift's story resonates as an enduring anthem, encouraging us to pursue our goals and embrace the transformative power of authenticity.

As we begin focusing on our goals, it's easy to feel overwhelmed, much like a juggler on a unicycle, pedaling furiously to keep all tasks and responsibilities airborne. The challenge, while daunting, is not insurmountable. The key lies in mastering the art of balance and maintaining a smooth flow amidst the chaos. This narrative is not just about overcoming obstacles; it's a guide to transforming the way we approach our goals, inspired by proven strategies and the wisdom of those who have mastered the art of productivity.

The cornerstone of this transformative journey is the recognition of the power of setting specific and challenging goals. Research published by the *Journal of Applied Psychology* underscores the significant improvement in workplace performance that such goals can instigate. They act as a beacon, guiding us through the fog of daily tasks, providing direction, accountability, and, crucially, motivation. However, identifying our biggest hurdles in staying motivated is just the starting point. Whether it's the constant firefighting or the pressure to prove our leadership skills, understanding these challenges is the first step toward overcoming them.

Our collective aim is to succeed not just in our careers but also in optimizing our time, improving our performance, driving change, and achieving a harmonious work-life balance. Yet, the path is riddled with obstacles. To navigate this path, we delve into key strategies: understanding personal motivation, setting specific and measurable goals, breaking goals into manageable tasks, employing tools to stay organized, and consistently monitoring progress. This approach doesn't just untangle the knot of chaos; it lays out a clear, achievable roadmap to our objectives.

Viewing motivation as a muscle that strengthens with use offers a new perspective. Neuroscience tells us that achieving goals triggers dopamine release, rewarding us with feelings of pleasure and satisfaction. This understanding shatters the myth that motivation precedes action, revealing that, in reality, taking even a small step can ignite motivation, creating a positive feedback loop powered by the progress principle.

The challenges of modern work, especially in remote settings, blur the lines between professional and personal life, making the principles of stress-free productivity, as outlined by David Allen in his GTD methodology, more relevant than ever. By externalizing tasks, breaking them down into actionable items, and trusting a system to free our minds, we can achieve a balance between productivity and relaxation, aligning our efforts with our natural energy cycles for maximum efficiency.

The Pomodoro Technique, leveraging short bursts of work followed by breaks, exemplifies how aligning with these cycles can boost productivity and motivation. Yet, the journey doesn't end with personal productivity. Writing down goals, as studies suggest, significantly increases the likelihood of success, transforming goal-setting from a task into a powerful habit.

By examining case studies like Google's implementation of Objectives and Key Results (OKRs), we see the practical application of these principles at an organizational level, demonstrating the universal applicability of these strategies. From identifying and articulating clear, measurable goals to breaking them down and systematically tackling each task, the process is a blueprint for achieving any objective.

"It's not about ideas. It's about making ideas happen." —Scott Belsky

The journey of Taylor Swift from a hopeful young talent to a global icon encapsulates the essence of what it takes to excel in portfolio and project management. Her story is not just about music; it's a masterclass in goal-setting, resilience, and strategic execution. Observing Swift's career, I see a mirror reflecting the qualities essential for managing complex projects and achieving strategic objectives.

Swift's early decision, supported by her family, to move to Nashville represents a strategic pivot—recognizing and seizing opportunities for growth. This is akin to the pivotal decisions we face in project management, where identifying and leveraging opportunities can set the course for success. The skepticism she faced due to her age and inexperience mirrors the doubts and challenges that often accompany new projects or innovative initiatives. Yet, Swift's response—to use criticism as fuel—teaches us the value of resilience and the power of a positive mindset in overcoming obstacles.

Her "aha" moment, realizing that conforming to industry norms was limiting her true potential, is a lesson in the importance of authenticity and innovation. In project management, this translates to the courage to deviate from conventional paths, to innovate, and to tailor approaches that best align with the unique needs of a project or an organization. Swift's transformation into a genre-defying artist underscores the need for flexibility and adaptability in managing projects, embracing change as a catalyst for growth.

My focus on the productivity superpower of setting specific and challenging goals is exemplified in Swift's methodical approach to her career. Her dedication to her craft, from exhaustive hours in the studio to meticulous planning of her marketing strategies, showcases the importance of a disciplined, goal-oriented approach. Just as Swift sets the bar high in her musical endeavors, we, too, must aim high in our projects, setting clear, measurable goals that challenge us to stretch beyond our comfort zones.

The application of strategies like the Pomodoro Technique and the principles of GTD (Getting Things Done) align with Swift's disciplined work ethic. These methodologies, emphasizing efficiency, focus, and the strategic breaking down of tasks, resonate with the structured yet flexible approach required in successful project management. They advocate for a balance between focused work and necessary breaks, optimizing productivity—principles that Swift seems to embody through her relentless yet strategically managed efforts.

Moreover, Swift's ability to connect deeply with her audience and build a loyal fanbase parallels the stakeholder engagement critical in project management. Just as she understands her audience's desires and expectations, effective project management involves engaging with stakeholders, understanding their needs, and ensuring projects align with overarching strategic goals.

Taylor Swift's journey offers profound insights into the art and science of project and portfolio management. Her story, viewed through the lens of my own experiences and perspectives on productivity and goal-setting, underscores the universal principles of strategic planning, resilience, adaptability, and stakeholder engagement. It teaches us that success in any field—be it music or project management—demands more than just talent or technical skills. It requires a focused dedication to goals, a willingness to embrace change, and the strategic execution of well-planned initiatives. Swift's narrative, intertwined with my commentary on productivity, serves as a beacon for aspiring professionals, guiding us toward achieving our own versions of success through the power of focus, resilience, and strategic action.

"You are never too old to set another goal or to dream a new dream."
—C.S. Lewis

"I've failed over and over and over again in my life. And that is why I succeed." —Michael Jordan

"You have to work hard to get your thinking clean to make it simple. But it's worth it in the end because once you get there, you can move mountains." —Steve Jobs

"People haven't always been there for me, but music always has. I stay focused on my goals, and I let the hard work speak for itself."
—Miley Cyrus (musician)

Am I clear about what my long-term goals are, and have I broken them down into actionable steps?

How do I maintain focus when distractions or setbacks occur?

What daily habits or routines help me stay committed to my goals?

How do I measure progress toward my goals to ensure I'm moving in the right direction?

Am I willing to make sacrifices in other areas of my life to achieve my most important goals?

How do I stay motivated when the journey toward my goals becomes difficult or tiring?

What strategies do I use to overcome procrastination and stay disciplined?

Do I frequently revisit and adjust my goals as I grow and change, or do I hold on to outdated objectives?

How do I balance short-term gratification with the long-term work required to reach my goals?

. . .

What resources or support systems do I rely on to help me stay focused and maintain momentum?

Taylor Swift's story offers valuable insights that can be translated into practical steps for effective project management. Let's distill these lessons into actionable strategies:

Step 1: Embrace Your Uniqueness

In project management, recognize that your team is composed of individuals with unique strengths. Embrace diversity and encourage team members to bring their distinctive skills to the table. Just as Taylor Swift transformed her music by embracing her uniqueness, project managers can leverage the diverse talents of their team for innovative solutions.

Rationale: Embracing diversity fosters creativity, resulting in a more robust and adaptable project team.

Step 2: Convert Challenges into Opportunities

Taylor Swift turned criticism and challenges into fuel for her artistic journey. Similarly, in project management, we view challenges as opportunities for growth. Encourage a mindset shift within the team, seeing obstacles as chances to innovate and improve processes.

Rationale: Transforming challenges into opportunities enhances team resilience and promotes a positive project environment.

Step 3: Foster Open Communication

Taylor's commitment to authenticity underscores the importance of open communication. In project management, create an environment where team members feel comfortable expressing ideas, concerns, and feedback. Foster a culture of transparent communication to enhance collaboration.

Rationale: Open communication ensures that all team members are aligned with project goals, minimizing misunderstandings and improving overall efficiency.

Step 4: Set Clear Goals
Taylor Swift's unwavering focus on her goals propelled her to global stardom. Apply this principle to project management by establishing clear, achievable objectives. Define project milestones, timelines, and key performance indicators to guide the team.

Rationale: Clearly defined goals provide a roadmap for the team, enhancing motivation and ensuring everyone is working toward a common purpose.

Step 5: Invest in Skill Development
Taylor's dedication to her craft involved continuous learning. In project management, invest in the professional development of your team. Provide training opportunities, workshops, and resources to enhance skills and keep abreast of industry trends.

Rationale: Ongoing skill development enhances team capabilities, contributing to the project's overall success.

Step 6: Encourage Innovation
Taylor Swift's willingness to evolve her musical style reflects a commitment to innovation. Similarly, in project management, a culture of innovation is fostered. Encourage team members to propose new ideas, technologies, or methodologies that can enhance project outcomes.

Rationale: Innovation drives efficiency and can lead to breakthroughs in project delivery, keeping the team at the forefront of industry best practices.

Step 7: Prioritize Work-Life Balance
Recognize the importance of balance in project management, just as Taylor values authenticity in her music. Avoid overloading team members with tasks, and ensure there's a healthy work-life equilibrium to prevent burnout.

Rationale: A balanced work environment fosters a positive team culture, improving morale and overall productivity.

By incorporating these practical steps inspired by Taylor Swift's journey, project managers can infuse creativity, resilience, and authenticity into their teams, fostering an environment conducive to project success.

Exercise 1: Uncover Team Talents
Objective: Embrace diversity within the team and uncover individual talents.
Steps:

1. Conduct a team-building session where members share their unique skills and experiences.
2. Create a skills inventory highlighting each team member's strengths.
3. Encourage collaboration by assigning tasks that align with team members' individual talents.
4. Reflect on how leveraging diverse skills enhances project outcomes.

Reflection Questions:

- How did recognizing and utilizing individual talents contribute to the success of the tasks?
- What strategies can be implemented to further integrate diverse skills into project activities?

Exercise 2: Transforming Challenges into Opportunities
Objective: Develop a mindset that views challenges as opportunities for growth.
Steps:

1. Identify recent challenges or setbacks in the project.
2. Brainstorm with the team on how each challenge can be reframed as an opportunity.

3. Implement one innovative solution derived from reframing a challenge.
4. Evaluate the impact of the solution on project efficiency.

Reflection Questions:

- How did transforming challenges into opportunities positively impact the team's morale?
- In what ways did reframing challenges lead to innovative problem-solving?

Exercise 3: Enhance Communication Strategies
Objective: Foster transparent and open communication within the team.
Steps:

1. Conduct a communication workshop emphasizing the importance of openness.
2. Implement a project communication plan that encourages regular updates and feedback.
3. Use collaboration tools to streamline communication and information sharing.
4. Evaluate the effectiveness of the new communication strategies.

Reflection Questions:

- How did transparent communication contribute to the team's understanding of project goals?
- What improvements can be made to further enhance communication within the team?

Exercise 4: Goal-Setting Workshop
Objective: Establish clear and achievable project goals.

Steps:

1. Facilitate a goal-setting workshop with the team to define project objectives.
2. Break down goals into smaller, achievable milestones.
3. Create a visual representation of the project roadmap.
4. Monitor progress regularly and celebrate achievements.

Reflection Questions:

- How did setting clear goals positively impact the team's focus and motivation?
- In what ways did breaking down goals into milestones improve project planning?

Exercise 5: Continuous Learning Initiative
Objective: Promote ongoing skill development among team members.
Steps:

1. Identify key skill areas relevant to the project and industry.
2. Provide access to training resources, workshops, or courses.
3. Encourage team members to share new insights and knowledge acquired.
4. Assess the impact of continuous learning on individual and team performance.

Reflection Questions:

- How did ongoing skill development contribute to individual and team capabilities?

- What mechanisms can be implemented to sustain a culture of continuous learning?

Exercise 6: Innovation Challenge
Objective: Cultivate a culture of innovation within the team.
Steps:

1. Initiate an innovation challenge where team members propose creative solutions to a project-related issue.
2. Implement one innovative idea generated during the challenge.
3. Evaluate the impact of the innovation on project efficiency and outcomes.
4. Recognize and reward innovative contributions.

Reflection Questions:

- How did fostering a culture of innovation contribute to the project's adaptability?
- In what ways did implementing innovative solutions enhance overall project performance?

Exercise 7: Work-Life Balance Assessment
Objective: Prioritize work-life balance to prevent burnout.
Steps:

1. Conduct a survey or team discussion to assess perceived work-life balance.
2. Implement strategies to promote a healthy work-life equilibrium.
3. Monitor team well-being and stress levels regularly.
4. Analyze the impact of work-life balance initiatives on team satisfaction and productivity.

Reflection Questions:

- How did prioritizing work-life balance contribute to team morale and satisfaction?
- What adjustments can be made to further enhance work-life balance within the team?

These step-by-step exercises, inspired by Taylor Swift's story, are designed to enhance various aspects of project management, including team collaboration, problem-solving, communication, goal setting, continuous learning, innovation, and well-being. Regularly incorporating these exercises can contribute to a dynamic and productive project management environment.

Resilience drives results. Discover weekly strategies to strengthen your mindset and maximize your potential:

Chapter 3
Beyoncé

Beyoncé's productivity superpower is her incredible work ethic.

"I'm a workaholic, and I don't believe in 'No.' If I'm not sleeping, nobody's sleeping. Put the time in, work hard, and everything else will follow." —Beyoncé

Productivity Smarts

In the fast-paced, high-stakes world of corporate project management, where efficiency and productivity are paramount, the story of Beyoncé Knowles stands as a shining example of what can be achieved through unyielding dedication and a relentless pursuit of excellence. Her journey from a young, ambitious girl in Houston, Texas, to becoming one of the most influential musicians of our time is a narrative that resonates deeply with anyone striving to excel in their career.

Beyoncé's story began with a dream. In her early days in Houston, her talent for singing and dancing was evident. She didn't just possess a natural ability; she was imbued with a drive to succeed that was rare for her age. This drive saw her working tirelessly, honing her skills, and pushing herself to the limits of her endurance. Even as a child, Beyoncé's focus was laser-sharp; she was not just playing at being a musician—she was laying the groundwork for a stellar career.

Throughout her journey, Beyoncé faced numerous challenges that would have derailed a lesser spirit. Rejections from record labels and criticism from the media were obstacles she encountered. Yet, these setbacks did not diminish her resolve; rather, they fueled her ambition, pushing her to work harder and aim higher. Her resilience in the face of these challenges is a crucial lesson for anyone navigating the competitive world of corporate projects.

A pivotal moment in Beyoncé's career was the realization that she needed to stop conforming to external expectations and start listening to her own inner voice. This moment of self-awareness marked a significant transformation in her career. She began creating music that was not only authentic and personal but also universally resonant. This authenticity is what has endeared her to millions of fans around the globe.

Beyoncé's work ethic is legendary. Known for her grueling hours in the studio and exhaustive rehearsal schedules, her commitment to her craft is a rarity. This incredible dedication has translated into remarkable achievements, including an astounding 32 Grammy Awards (and 99 nominations) and over 200 million records sold worldwide. Her meticulous attention to detail and refusal to settle for anything less than perfection are qualities that anyone in a high-pressure, results-driven environment can aspire to emulate.

Beyond her musical career, Beyoncé's influence extends into social advocacy. She uses her platform to champion causes of social justice and equality, demonstrating that success brings with it a responsibility to make a positive impact on the world. She stands as a role model not just for aspiring musicians but for anyone looking to leverage their professional success for the greater good.

Influenced by the likes of Michael Jackson and Whitney Houston, Beyoncé has carved out her own unique place in cultural history. Her journey is a testament to the power of passion, hard work, and an unwavering belief in one's own abilities. For the corporate professional juggling deadlines, managing teams, and striving for excellence, Beyoncé's story is a beacon of inspiration. It teaches us that with enough dedication and perseverance, we can overcome any obstacle, achieve our most ambitious goals, and, perhaps most importantly, remain true to our authentic selves in the process.

Beyoncé's narrative is more than a tale of musical success; it's a blueprint for anyone striving to achieve greatness in their field. Her story encourages us to embrace our inner drive, to work tirelessly in the face of challenges, and to never lose sight of our dreams. With determination, perseverance, and a commitment to authenticity, we, too, can reach the pinnacle of our professions and make a lasting, positive mark on the world.

The quest for continuous improvement and enhanced productivity is a universal challenge. Drawing inspiration from both historical successes and modern methodologies, the Kaizen method emerges as a powerful tool in this quest. Rooted in the Japanese philosophy of continuous improvement, Kaizen offers a pathway to achieving personal and professional excellence by embracing small, incremental changes. My journey, like that of many professionals striving for efficiency and effectiveness, has been profoundly influenced by the principles of Kaizen.

The revelation that multitasking diminishes productivity and increases stress was a pivotal moment in my quest for improved work performance. This understanding led me to explore alternative approaches to managing workloads and optimizing processes. The Kaizen method, with its focus on gradual improvement, provided the blueprint I needed to transform my work habits and, ultimately, my outcomes.

The essence of Kaizen lies in its simplicity and its profound impact on productivity. By grouping similar tasks and dedicating focused time to each batch, I discovered a more efficient way to manage my responsibilities. This approach not only streamlined my workflow but also significantly enhanced the quality of my output. It was akin to the meticulous preparation of a chef who, by focusing on one dish at a time, ensures each ingredient complements the other, resulting in a culinary masterpiece.

Implementing the Kaizen method in my work processes began with evaluating my current productivity levels. Utilizing a productivity evaluation worksheet, I identified areas requiring improvement and set about making small, incremental changes. This process was both enlightening and empowering. It revealed that the path to significant improvement does not necessarily require radical changes but rather a series of small, manageable steps that cumulatively lead to substantial gains.

The benefits of adopting the Kaizen method were immediately apparent. An increase in productivity, a reduction in stress, and an improvement in the quality of my work were just the beginning. Studies corroborating these results abound, with companies reporting an average productivity increase of 25% upon implementing Kaizen principles. Beyond the metrics, the method fostered an environment of continuous learning and adaptation, where every challenge became an opportunity for improvement.

The journey toward implementing Kaizen was not without its

obstacles. Resistance to change, especially in established routines, posed a significant challenge. However, by fostering a culture of open communication and collective effort toward common goals, these hurdles were gradually overcome. The Kaizen method transcends the individual, promoting a collective ethos of improvement that benefits the entire organization.

Experts like Masakai Amani have extensively documented the transformative power of Kaizen in various industries. From manufacturing giants like Toyota to healthcare institutions, the method has been instrumental in driving efficiency, reducing waste, and enhancing customer satisfaction. These examples serve as a testament to the versatility and effectiveness of Kaizen, offering valuable insights and practical strategies for its implementation.

In today's fast-paced and competitive work environment, the importance of continuously improving and staying ahead cannot be overstated. The Kaizen method provides a structured yet flexible framework for achieving this, emphasizing the value of small changes and the power of cumulative impact. It challenges the traditional notion of productivity, shifting the focus from working longer hours to working smarter.

Incorporating the Kaizen method into my work processes has been transformative. It has not only improved my productivity and efficiency but has also instilled a mindset of continuous improvement. The Kaizen method, with its focus on small, incremental changes, offers a practical and effective approach to enhancing work processes and achieving professional excellence. It reminds us that the path to greatness is paved with small steps, each one bringing us closer to our goals. In embracing Kaizen, we embrace a culture of continuous improvement, setting the stage for a lifetime of achievement and success.

"Dreams don't work unless you do." —John C. Maxwell

. . .

Work ethic and productivity exemplified by Beyoncé Knowles, intertwined with the disciplined approach of the Kaizen method, provide a compelling blueprint for success. Beyoncé's meteoric rise from young talent in Houston to a global music icon mirrors the journey many project managers undertake—navigating challenges, optimizing processes, and relentlessly pursuing excellence.

Beyoncé's story is not just about her incredible talent; it's about her extraordinary work ethic, her commitment to continuous improvement, and her ability to remain focused and productive amidst the pressures of fame. This dedication, as mirrored in the corporate world, underscores the importance of a strong work ethic and productivity in achieving project goals. Her journey teaches us that success is not a product of luck but the result of hard work, perseverance, and an unwavering commitment to excellence.

Similarly, the Kaizen method, with its emphasis on continuous, incremental improvement, offers a structured approach to enhancing productivity and efficiency in project management. By adopting this methodology, professionals can cultivate a culture of continuous improvement, where small, consistent changes lead to significant improvements over time. This approach aligns with the meticulous preparation and focus seen in Beyoncé's work ethic, where every detail is given attention, and every performance is an opportunity for refinement.

The blending of Beyoncé's narrative with the Kaizen philosophy highlights a crucial lesson for portfolio and project managers: the path to achieving project objectives and career success is paved with dedication, a strong work ethic, and a commitment to continuous improvement. Beyoncé's journey demonstrates that with enough dedication and perseverance, overcoming any obstacle and achieving our most ambitious goals is possible. Similarly, the Kaizen method teaches us that incremental changes, when consistently applied, can lead to substantial improvements in productivity, quality, and efficiency.

In the realm of project management, where deadlines are tight and expectations high, the principles embodied by Beyoncé and the Kaizen method serve as a guide. They remind us that success requires more than just talent or knowledge; it demands a relentless pursuit of improvement, an unwavering focus on productivity, and a work ethic that does not shy away from challenges.

Implementing the Kaizen method in project management processes, much like incorporating Beyoncé's work ethic into one's professional life, begins with a commitment to excellence. It involves regularly evaluating and refining processes, embracing small steps toward improvement, and fostering a culture that values feedback and collaboration. This methodological approach, combined with the inspiration drawn from Beyoncé's career, encourages project managers to strive for excellence in every aspect of their work.

The synthesis of Beyoncé's unparalleled dedication to her craft and the disciplined, incremental approach of the Kaizen method offers a compelling framework for success in portfolio and project management. This narrative not only inspires but also provides a practical roadmap for achieving excellence, demonstrating that with the right work ethic, productivity strategies, and commitment to continuous improvement, reaching the pinnacle of professional achievement is within reach.

> "I've learned that anything in life worth having comes from patience and hard work." —Greg Behrendt

> "There are no secrets to success. It is the result of preparation, hard work, and learning from failure." —Colin Powell

"The difference between ordinary and extraordinary is that little extra." —Jimmy Johnson

"Work hard in silence, let success make the noise." —Frank Ocean (musician)

"Dreams don't work unless you do." —John C. Maxwell

How do I define a strong work ethic, and do my actions align with that definition?

Am I putting in the necessary effort to achieve my goals, or am I relying on shortcuts?

How do I stay motivated during challenging or monotonous tasks?

Do I take pride in my work, and how does that impact my level of effort?

What daily habits contribute to or hinder my productivity?

How do I handle setbacks, and do I use them as opportunities to strengthen my work ethic?

Am I consistent in my work performance, or do I only work hard when I feel inspired?

How do I balance hard work with the need for rest and avoiding burnout?

Do I hold myself accountable for both my successes and failures in my work?

How do I continuously seek improvement and refine my skills to ensure long-term success?

Inspired by Beyoncé's incredible journey, project managers can adopt several practical steps to integrate her exemplary work ethic, dedication, and innovative spirit into their project management practices. Here are key steps to follow:

1. **Cultivate Passion and Drive:**
    - Encourage team members to find aspects of the project they are passionate about.
    - Foster an environment where enthusiasm and commitment are recognized and appreciated.
2. **Set High Standards for Excellence:**
    - Like Beyoncé's commitment to perfection, establish high standards for all project deliverables.
    - Regularly review and assess the quality of work, ensuring it aligns with these high standards.
3. **Embrace Authenticity and Individuality:**
    - Encourage team members to bring their unique perspectives and strengths to the project.
    - Create a culture where diverse ideas and approaches are valued and integrated into the project's strategy.
4. **Foster Resilience and Perseverance:**

- Teach the team to view challenges as opportunities for growth and innovation.
- Develop strategies to effectively manage and overcome setbacks, keeping the team motivated and focused.

5. **Encourage Continuous Improvement:**
   - Like Beyoncé's constant evolution, it promotes a culture of continuous learning and development.
   - Provide opportunities for team members to enhance their skills and apply them to the project.

6. **Promote Effective Communication:**
   - Ensure clear and open communication within the team, fostering collaboration and mutual understanding.
   - Use diverse communication channels to keep all team members informed and engaged.

7. **Balance Hard Work with Well-Being:**
   - Advocate for a healthy work-life balance to maintain high levels of energy and prevent burnout.
   - Encourage mindfulness and well-being practices to support the team's physical and mental health.

8. **Innovate and Take Calculated Risks:**
   - Encourage the team to explore new methods and solutions, much like Beyoncé's innovative approaches in her career.
   - Create a safe space for taking calculated risks and learning from both successes and failures.

9. **Lead with Empathy and Understanding:**
   - Recognize the individual needs and challenges of each team member, offering support and guidance.
   - Foster a team culture of empathy where members feel valued and understood.

10. **Celebrate Achievements and Milestones:**

- Acknowledge and celebrate both individual and team achievements.
- Use these celebrations to motivate and inspire the team toward future success.

By incorporating these steps, project managers can create a dynamic and effective team environment that mirrors Beyoncé's dedication, creativity, and resilience, leading to enhanced project success and team cohesion.

To harness the exceptional work ethic and dedication exemplified by Beyoncé in the context of project management, you can implement a series of step-by-step exercises with your team. These exercises are designed to promote passion, dedication, high standards, and resilience, mirroring the qualities that have contributed to Beyoncé's phenomenal success.

Exercise 1: Discovering Passion in Projects

Objective: Help team members identify and align their passions with project goals.

- **Step 1:** Have each team member list aspects of the project that excite or interest them.
- **Step 2:** Discuss as a group how these interests can enhance their roles and contributions to the project.
- **Step 3:** Develop action plans for each member to integrate their passions into their daily tasks.

Exercise 2: Setting and Upholding High Standards

Objective: Establish and maintain high-quality standards within the project.

- **Step 1:** Conduct a workshop to define what high quality means in the context of your project.

- **Step 2:** Develop measurable quality standards and criteria.
- **Step 3:** Implement a regular review process to ensure these standards are consistently met.

Exercise 3: Embracing Authenticity and Individuality

Objective: Encourage unique contributions and diverse perspectives in the project.

- **Step 1:** Host a session where each team member shares something unique about their skills or background.
- **Step 2:** Brainstorm ways to utilize these diverse skills in the project.
- **Step 3:** Implement strategies that allow individual strengths to be used effectively in the project.

Exercise 4: Building Resilience Through Role-Playing

Objective: Enhance the team's ability to adapt and overcome challenges.

- **Step 1:** Present hypothetical challenging scenarios related to the project.
- **Step 2:** Role-play these scenarios in small groups, focusing on developing resilience and finding solutions.
- **Step 3:** Debrief and discuss what strategies were effective and how they can be applied in real situations.

Exercise 5: Continuous Learning and Development

Objective: Promote ongoing skill enhancement and learning.

- **Step 1:** Identify key skills or knowledge areas beneficial for the project.

- **Step 2:** Organize training sessions or allocate time for self-guided learning.
- **Step 3:** Encourage team members to share new learnings and how they can be applied to the project.

Exercise 6: Effective Communication Workshop
Objective: Improve communication skills and collaboration within the team.

- **Step 1:** Organize a workshop on effective communication techniques, including active listening and clear articulation.
- **Step 2:** Engage in practical exercises, such as group discussions or presentations, to practice these skills.
- **Step 3:** Implement a structured communication protocol for the project.

Exercise 7: Balancing Work and Well-Being
Objective: Ensure a healthy balance between hard work and personal well-being.

- **Step 1:** Conduct a session on the importance of work-life balance and its impact on productivity.
- **Step 2:** Share strategies and tools for managing workloads effectively.
- **Step 3:** Encourage team members to set personal goals for maintaining balance.

Exercise 8: Encouraging Innovation and Risk-Taking
Objective: Foster a culture where innovative thinking and calculated risks are encouraged.

- **Step 1:** Share examples of successful innovation in your industry.
- **Step 2:** Brainstorm with the team on potential innovative approaches to current project challenges.
- **Step 3:** Evaluate these ideas and discuss how to safely implement them.

Exercise 9: Empathetic Leadership and Support
Objective: Create an empathetic and supportive team environment.

- **Step 1:** Facilitate a roundtable for team members to share personal challenges or concerns.
- **Step 2:** Work together to find solutions or offer support.
- **Step 3:** Establish a regular check-in routine to maintain a supportive environment.

Exercise 10: Recognizing and Celebrating Achievements
Objective: Acknowledge hard work and celebrate achievements.

- **Step 1:** Identify recent successes or milestones in the project.
- **Step 2:** Organize a team event or acknowledgment to celebrate these achievements.
- **Step 3:** Encourage team members to share their contributions and learn from these successes.

These exercises can help project teams develop a strong work ethic, foster a culture of continuous improvement, and enhance collaboration and communication, ultimately leading to more successful project outcomes.

Learn how to align your time and energy with what matters most —sign up for free weekly tips here:

Part Two

Pillar Two – Reinvention and Innovation

The Lifeblood of Longevity

Reinvention and innovation are the forces that keep creativity alive and success enduring. In a world that evolves at an accelerating pace, resting on past achievements is not an option. Reinvention ensures relevance, while innovation drives progress. Together, they create a cycle of renewal that allows individuals and organizations to thrive in changing landscapes. These qualities require courage, adaptability, and a willingness to step outside of comfort zones to embrace new possibilities.

Reinvention is not merely about change for its own sake; it's about growth. It's the art of recognizing when transformation is necessary and having the vision to pursue it boldly. Innovation, meanwhile, fuels reinvention by challenging norms, experimenting with fresh ideas, and finding better ways to solve problems. Both are essential for staying ahead in an environment where stagnation can mean obsolescence.

Few artists have embodied these principles as powerfully as David Bowie, the Beatles, and Ed Sheeran. Each of these icons reshaped their industries by reinventing themselves and innovating relentlessly, leaving legacies that continue to inspire. Their practices offer valuable lessons for anyone seeking to stay relevant, creative, and prolific in their work.

David Bowie was a master of reinvention. Throughout his career, he transformed himself again and again, adopting personas like Ziggy Stardust, Thin White Duke, and others that not only reflected the times but also shaped them. Bowie's ability to anticipate change and adapt to it was key to his longevity. He didn't wait for the world to catch up to him; he reinvented himself to stay ahead of it. For Bowie, reinvention wasn't just about appearances—it was about evolving his sound, his approach, and his message to remain a cultural force.

The Beatles, by contrast, revolutionized music through relentless innovation. From pioneering new recording techniques to experimenting with diverse musical styles, they continually pushed the boundaries of what was possible in their craft. The Beatles didn't settle for repetition or predictability; instead, they embraced change, challenging themselves and their listeners to explore uncharted territories. Their willingness to experiment redefined what music could be and established a culture of creativity that still influences artists today.

Ed Sheeran offers yet another perspective on reinvention and innovation: structured creativity. While Sheeran may not adopt personas or radically alter genres, his prolific songwriting output demonstrates a commitment to innovation within a disciplined framework. Sheeran's ability to consistently produce quality work stems from his systems—structured processes that allow him to channel creativity efficiently without sacrificing originality. His approach shows that innovation doesn't always have to be disruptive; it can also be about refining systems to maximize productivity.

The lessons from these icons highlight the importance of reinvention and innovation in any field. Bowie teaches us to embrace transformation as a tool for staying relevant. The Beatles remind us to foster a culture of experimentation where new ideas can flourish.

Productivity Smarts

Sheeran shows us the power of creating systems that support consistent creativity. Together, their practices provide a roadmap for navigating the challenges of change and driving progress in the workplace.

As you delve into this pillar, consider how reinvention and innovation apply to your own professional context. Are you adapting to the changes in your industry? Are you encouraging experimentation within your team? Have you built systems that allow you to innovate consistently? These questions can guide you toward creating an environment where reinvention and innovation become second nature.

In the chapters ahead, we'll explore how to integrate these principles into your work. From embracing transformation to fostering creativity and building systems for productivity, you'll gain practical insights into how reinvention and innovation can propel you forward. Whether you're leading a team, managing a project, or pursuing personal growth, this pillar will equip you to stay relevant, adaptable, and consistently creative.

Reinvention and innovation are not just the keys to survival; they are the pathways to greatness. With inspiration from Bowie, the Beatles, and Sheeran, you'll discover how to transform challenges into opportunities, push boundaries, and leave a legacy that endures.

Chapter 4
David Bowie

David Bowie's productivity superpower was his ability to reinvent himself constantly.

"I reinvented my image so many times that I'm in denial that I was originally an overweight Korean woman." —David Bowie

Gerald J. Leonard

In the landscape of modern music, David Bowie stands as a colossus, a figure emblematic of creativity, reinvention, and enduring influence. For ambitious professionals and creatives alike, Bowie's life is a blueprint of how relentless innovation and adaptability can lead to lasting success.

Born in Brixton, London, in 1947, Bowie was brought up in a working-class family steeped in the dynamic and diverse music scene of 1960s London. This melting pot of cultural influences played a pivotal role in shaping his early musical experiences. Despite the humble beginnings, Bowie's fascination with music was apparent from a young age, as he swiftly garnered a reputation as a talented and versatile musician.

Bowie's journey to stardom was not without its hurdles. In his early career, he grappled with finding a distinct musical identity, often finding himself eclipsed by his contemporaries. Yet, it was his unyielding spirit and refusal to succumb to these challenges that set the stage for his remarkable transformation.

The early 1970s marked a significant turning point for Bowie. The creation of Ziggy Stardust, a flamboyant androgynous alter ego, was more than an artistic shift; it was a declaration of his creative liberation. This period saw Bowie blending various musical styles, from rock to electronic, and creating an avant-garde sound that shattered conventional norms. Ziggy Stardust was not just a character but a symbol of Bowie's ingenuity and his ability to transcend traditional boundaries.

Bowie's greatest strength lay in his ability to continually reinvent himself. His adaptability was his productivity superpower, enabling him to traverse a spectrum of musical styles and personas. From his soulful Thin White Duke persona to the experimental sounds of the Berlin era, Bowie's career was a kaleidoscope of ever-evolving artistry. This constant reinvention kept him relevant and influential, a feat few artists have managed to achieve.

Throughout his illustrious career, Bowie released 27 studio albums and sold over 140 million records worldwide, a testament to his widespread appeal and impact. His theatrical performances and unique fashion sense transcended music, influencing popular culture and fashion. Bowie was not just a musician; he was an icon, a trendsetter who reshaped the cultural landscape.

Bowie's artistry was deeply influenced by the work of Andy Warhol and the Velvet Underground. His collaboration with Lou Reed exemplifies his ability to connect and create with artists across different genres, further showcasing his versatility and openness to diverse influences.

David Bowie's unbridled belief in the power of creativity and self-expression offers invaluable lessons. His willingness to experiment, take risks, and break new ground serves as a guide for professionals in any field. Bowie's life encourages us to embrace our uniqueness, push beyond our comfort zones, and continually seek new ways to express and redefine ourselves.

The story of David Bowie is more than a tale of musical triumph; it's a narrative of transformation, resilience, and the relentless pursuit of artistic evolution. His journey inspires us to adopt a mindset of constant growth and reinvention. As we reflect on Bowie's extraordinary life, let us imbibe the essence of his creative spirit: to be fearless, innovative, and always in motion. Bowie's legacy is a clarion call to embrace change, celebrate our individuality, and pursue our passions with unwavering dedication.

In the relentless pursuit of productivity and success, the journey of transformation is often underscored by moments of introspection and radical change. The story of Mary, a program manager I once had the honor of mentoring, exemplifies the essence of reinvention and the pivotal role of adapting innovative strategies to navigate the complexities of professional and personal life. Mary found herself entangled in a labyrinth of simultaneous projects and responsibilities, each demanding her attention and stretching her to her limits. The stress and overwhelm became her constant companions, clouding her vision and diminishing her effectiveness. It was during this tumultuous period that the concept of time blocking was introduced to her—a practice that promised to reclaim the lost control over her sprawling schedule. The transformation was nothing short of remarkable. By segmenting her day into dedicated blocks of time, each earmarked for specific tasks, Mary was able to channel her focus and energies more efficiently. This wasn't just about managing time; it was about prioritizing her life's goals and aligning her daily actions with them. The result was a profound uplift in her productivity, a significant reduction in stress, and an overall improvement in her performance. This metamorphosis of Mary's approach to work and life mirrors the broader narrative of reinventing oneself in the face of adversity. It underscores the power of embracing change and the importance of innovative practices in unlocking our full potential. Time blocking, as demonstrated by successful figures like Elon Musk, Tim Ferriss, and Gary Vaynerchuk, is more than a productivity hack; it's a testament to the efficacy of disciplined focus and the strategic allocation of our most precious resource: time.

The journey of reinvention, as illustrated by Mary's story, is a compelling reminder of our capacity for growth and transformation. It challenges us to question the status quo to seek out and adopt practices that propel us toward our goals. Time blocking, in this context, emerges not just as a tool for managing tasks but as a philosophy for living a more intentional and fulfilling life. As we navigate the complexities of our careers and personal lives, the story of Mary serves as a beacon, illuminating the path to productivity and success through the power of change and reinvention. It invites us to explore the boundaries of our potential and embrace the practices that can lead us to achieve greater satisfaction and fulfillment in all facets of our lives. So, as we ponder upon the steps to implement time blocking or any other transformative practice, let us remember that the essence of productivity lies not in the mere completion of tasks but in the continuous journey of self-improvement and the relentless pursuit of our highest aspirations.

Productivity Smarts

"When I let go of what I am, I become what I might be." —Lao Tzu

The essence of reinvention, particularly in the domain of portfolio management, mirrors the transformative journey of iconic figures like David Bowie in the realm of music. Just as Bowie's career was marked by continual evolution and adaptability, portfolio managers must also embrace change and innovation to thrive in the ever-shifting landscape of business and investment.

David Bowie's journey from a young musician in Brixton to an international superstar is a testament to the power of reinvention. His ability to adapt and transform himself, from the androgynous Ziggy Stardust to the soulful Thin White Duke, not only kept him relevant but also cemented his status as a trailblazer in the music industry. This capacity for change, for shedding the old and embracing the new, is equally critical in portfolio management.

In the fast-paced world of business, markets evolve, technologies advance, and consumer behaviors shift with dizzying speed. Portfolio managers, much like Bowie, cannot afford to remain static. The strategies and investments that yielded success yesterday may not do so tomorrow. Therefore, the ability to anticipate changes, adapt strategies, and even pivot when necessary becomes indispensable.

Let's consider the narrative of Mary, a program manager whose story exemplifies the practical application of reinvention in a professional setting. Overwhelmed by the sheer volume of projects and the stress they entailed, Mary found herself at a crossroads. The introduction of time blocking as a strategy was her Ziggy Stardust moment —her leap into a new way of working that radically transformed her productivity and overall well-being. Through this reinvention of her approach to time management, Mary was able to prioritize, focus, and achieve a level of success she previously thought was unattainable.

For portfolio managers, the lesson is clear. Embracing innovative strategies such as time blocking, diversification, or even exploring new markets and investment vehicles can be transformative. It requires a willingness to experiment, to take calculated risks, and to learn from both successes and failures. Just as Bowie drew inspiration from a wide array of sources—from music to art to literature—portfolio managers should also look beyond traditional sources for insights and strategies that can drive growth and resilience.

Moreover, Bowie's influence extended far beyond his music. He was a cultural icon whose impact was felt in fashion, film, and even finance, where his pioneering use of "Bowie Bonds" introduced a new way of thinking about the value of music as an asset. Similarly, portfolio managers have the potential to influence not just the financial performance of their portfolios but also the broader strategic direction of their organizations. By championing innovation and embracing change, they can lead their teams and companies to new heights.

In conclusion, the narrative of reinvention, illustrated through the lives of David Bowie and Mary, offers powerful lessons for portfolio managers. It teaches us the value of adaptability, the importance of continually seeking out new ideas and strategies, and the courage to embrace change. As we navigate the complexities of the modern business world, let us take inspiration from these stories and strive to reinvent ourselves and our approaches to portfolio management, ensuring that we remain ahead of the curve and achieve lasting success.

"One thing about me is that I'm very much like the Black Madonna. I love to reinvent myself, and that's because I am a very free person." — Lil' Kim

"When I let go of what I am, I become what I might be." —Lao Tzu

"When I make a film, I am hoping to reinvent the genre a little bit. I just do it my way. I make my own little Quentin versions of them... I consider myself a student of cinema. It's almost like I am going for my professorship in cinema, and the day I die is the day I graduate. It is a lifelong study." —Quentin Tarantino

"I'm a multidimensional person, and that's the freedom of fashion: that you're able to reinvent yourself through how you dress and how you cut your hair or whatever." —Emma Watson

"I liked pretending to be other people: I could reinvent myself, reinvent my own reality." —Helena Bonham Carter

What aspects of your current identity or habits are holding you back from achieving your potential?

Are these rooted in external expectations or internal limitations?

What does the ideal version of yourself look like in terms of skills, mindset, and behavior?

What steps can you take today to move closer to that vision?

How do you navigate the fear of failure or judgment when trying to reinvent yourself?

What strategies can you use to overcome these fears?

What areas of your life—personal, professional, or emotional—are most in need of transformation?

What small changes can you implement immediately to start the process?

How do you balance maintaining your core values while adopting new skills or perspectives?

What are the non-negotiable aspects of your identity that you want to keep intact?

What external influences (e.g., mentors, books, experiences) can help guide you in your reinvention?

Are there people or resources you haven't yet explored that could offer fresh perspectives?

How do you stay adaptable and open to change while committing to reinventing yourself?

How can you remain flexible and resilient when facing unexpected challenges?

What old habits or beliefs need to be discarded for you to evolve into the next version of yourself?

Are there any lingering self-limiting beliefs you haven't yet confronted?

What specific milestones or markers will indicate that your reinvention is successful?

How will you measure progress along the way to ensure you stay on track?

How do you handle relationships or environments that may resist or hinder your reinvention?

What boundaries or communication strategies can help you manage this resistance?

David Bowie's extraordinary journey of continuous reinvention and adaptation offers invaluable lessons for project management. By emulating his approach, project managers can foster a culture of innovation and adaptability in their teams. Here are practical steps to integrate the essence of Bowie's career into project management:

1. Foster a Culture of Continuous Innovation

- **Encourage Creative Thinking:** Like Bowie, encourage team members to think creatively and propose innovative solutions.

- **Regular Brainstorming Sessions:** Organize sessions where team members can freely express new ideas and concepts.

2. Embrace Change and Adaptability

- **Flexible Project Planning:** Develop project plans that are adaptable to change, mirroring Bowie's ability to evolve with the times.
- **Encourage Agility:** Train the team in agile methodologies, emphasizing the importance of adaptability in project execution.

3. Cultivate Diverse and Inclusive Team Environments

- **Diverse Team Composition:** Assemble a team with diverse backgrounds and skill sets, reflecting Bowie's wide range of musical influences.
- **Inclusive Decision Making:** Ensure that every team member has a voice in the decision-making process.

4. Encourage Risk-Taking Within Safe Boundaries

- **Calculated Risk-Taking:** Promote a culture where taking calculated risks is encouraged, but with a clear understanding of potential impacts.
- **Learn from Failures:** Create an environment where failure is seen as a learning opportunity, not a setback.

5. Develop Personal and Professional Growth

- **Continuous Learning:** Encourage team members to

pursue continuous learning and development, reflecting Bowie's lifelong pursuit of musical mastery.
- **Skill Development Workshops:** Offer workshops and training sessions that help team members acquire new skills.

6. Promote Individuality and Personal Branding

- **Unique Contributions:** Recognize and value the unique contributions of each team member, much like Bowie's unique contributions to music.
- **Encourage Personal Branding:** Motivate team members to develop their personal brand within the team, fostering a sense of ownership and pride in their work.

7. Implement Change and Transformations

- **Change Management:** Develop a robust change management process, helping the team to navigate and embrace change effectively.
- **Transformational Leadership:** Practice transformational leadership that motivates and inspires team members to embrace new challenges.

8. Provide Regular Feedback and Iterative Improvements

- **Feedback Mechanisms:** Establish regular feedback channels to continuously improve processes and outcomes.
- **Iterative Development:** Implement iterative development processes, allowing for continuous improvements based on feedback.

9. Balance Creativity with Practicality

- **Creative Solutions:** Encourage creative solutions to project challenges while ensuring they remain practical and feasible.
- **Resource Management:** Balance creativity with effective resource management, ensuring project goals are met efficiently.

10. Celebrate Success and Innovation

- **Recognize Achievements:** Celebrate milestones and innovative solutions developed by the team.
- **Sharing Success Stories:** Share success stories within the organization to inspire others.

By integrating these steps into project management, teams can channel the innovative spirit of David Bowie, driving projects forward with creativity, adaptability, and a forward-thinking approach.

To channel the innovative and adaptive spirit of David Bowie into project management, here are step-by-step exercises that can help teams embrace change, foster creativity, and promote continuous learning:

Exercise 1: Creative Ideation Workshop

Objective: Encourage creative thinking and innovation within the team.

- **Step 1:** Introduce a current project challenge and ask for unconventional solutions.
- **Step 2:** Conduct a brainstorming session, encouraging wild and creative ideas.
- **Step 3:** Evaluate the ideas and discuss how they can be realistically implemented.

Exercise 2: Adaptability Role Play
Objective: Enhance the team's ability to adapt to unexpected changes.

- **Step 1:** Create a scenario where a major change affects the project.
- **Step 2:** Divide the team into groups and have them role-play their response to the change.
- **Step 3:** Discuss the different approaches and identify key learning points.

Exercise 3: Diversity and Inclusion Activity
Objective: Celebrate and leverage the diverse backgrounds of the team.

- **Step 1:** Have each team member share something unique about their background or skills.
- **Step 2:** Discuss how these diverse elements can contribute to the project.
- **Step 3:** Identify practical ways to incorporate this diversity into the project workflow.

Exercise 4: Risk-Taking and Learning from Failure
Objective: Foster a culture where calculated risk-taking is encouraged.

- **Step 1:** Ask team members to share past experiences where taking a risk led to either success or failure.
- **Step 2:** Analyze what was learned from these experiences.
- **Step 3:** Discuss how these lessons can be applied to current or future projects.

Exercise 5: Continuous Learning Challenge

Objective: Promote ongoing skill development and learning.

- **Step 1:** Assign a new tool or skill relevant to the project for the team to learn.
- **Step 2:** Set a timeframe for learning and applying this new skill.
- **Step 3:** Share experiences and challenges faced during the learning process.

Exercise 6: Personal Branding Workshop

Objective: Encourage team members to develop and express their unique strengths.

- **Step 1:** Conduct a workshop on personal branding and its importance in a professional setting.
- **Step 2:** Have each team member identify their unique strengths and how they can be utilized in the project.
- **Step 3:** Develop action plans for each team member to apply their strengths to the project.

Exercise 7: Change Management Simulation

Objective: Improve the team's ability to manage and respond to change.

- **Step 1:** Simulate a major change in project direction or scope.
- **Step 2:** Task teams to develop a plan to manage this change.
- **Step 3:** Review and critique the plans, focusing on adaptability and resourcefulness.

Exercise 8: Feedback and Improvement Session

Objective: Create a culture of continuous improvement through feedback.

- **Step 1:** Implement a regular session where team members can give and receive constructive feedback on project work.
- **Step 2:** Discuss how this feedback can be used for personal and project improvement.
- **Step 3:** Establish action items based on the feedback.

Exercise 9: Balancing Creativity and Practicality

Objective: Find a balance between innovative ideas and realistic project execution.

- **Step 1:** Present a project issue that requires a creative yet practical solution.
- **Step 2:** Brainstorm creative solutions, then refine them to ensure practicality and feasibility.
- **Step 3:** Evaluate and select the best solutions to be implemented in the project.

Exercise 10: Success Celebration

Objective: Recognize and celebrate the team's achievements and innovations.

- **Step 1:** Identify recent project successes or innovative solutions developed by the team.
- **Step 2:** Organize a team celebration to acknowledge these achievements.
- **Step 3:** Share success stories with the wider organization to inspire others.

By regularly engaging in these exercises, project teams can foster a culture of creativity, adaptability, and continuous learning, mirroring the dynamic and innovative spirit of David Bowie.

Gerald J. Leonard

Gain practical techniques to eliminate distractions and supercharge your focus—join today:

Chapter 5

The Beatles

hile I thought that I was learning how to live, I have been learning how to collaborate." —John Lennon

Growing up in Liverpool in the 1950s, John Lennon, Paul McCartney, George Harrison, and Ringo Starr were just like any other teenagers. They loved music, played in local bands, and dreamed of making it big one day. But little did they know that they were about to change the world.

The early days of the Beatles were humble, characterized by a

shared love for music and a spirit of teamwork. Lennon and McCartney's songwriting partnership quickly became the core of their sound, a fusion of distinct styles that captivated their growing audience. Each member brought something unique to the table: McCartney's melodic intuition, Lennon's lyrical depth, Harrison's innovative guitar techniques, and Starr's rhythmic precision. Together, they crafted a sound that was more than just a sum of its parts.

Their "aha" moment came in 1963 when they released their first album, *Please Please Me*. It was an instant success, reaching number one on the charts and launching them into stardom. The Beatles had discovered their unique sound, blending rock and roll with pop, and the world couldn't get enough of it.

As the Beatles soared to international fame, their collaborative dynamic evolved. They were no longer just a band; they were a unified force of musical innovation. Their studio years, notably during the creation of groundbreaking albums like *Revolver* and *Sgt. Pepper's Lonely Hearts Club Band*, marked the zenith of this innovation. The studio became their canvas, where they experimented with multi-track recording, embraced unconventional instruments, and pushed the boundaries of music production.

The heart of the Beatles' innovation lay in the legendary songwriting partnership of Lennon and McCartney. This collaboration produced some of the most iconic songs in music history. "Come Together," "Hey Jude," "Lucy in the Sky with Diamonds," and so many others were not just songs; they were collaborative masterpieces that defined a generation.

The 1960s were a time of rapid change, both socially and culturally, and the Beatles mirrored this evolution in their music. They seamlessly moved through genres, from folk-rock to psychedelic pop, always staying ahead of the curve and redefining the soundscape of popular music.

When the Beatles disbanded in 1970, it was not the end but a new beginning. Their influence on music and culture has remained unparalleled. They left behind a legacy that continues to inspire musicians and bands worldwide, a legacy that proves the enduring power of teamwork, creativity, and the willingness to innovate.

Decades on, the music of the Beatles still resonates with the harmony of collaboration and innovation. Their journey, from a local band in Liverpool to global icons, is a reminder that when individuals come together with a shared vision and a willingness to experiment, they can create something truly timeless—a symphony that echoes across generations.

So, what was their productivity superpower? It was their ability to collaborate and innovate. The Beatles were constantly experimenting with new sounds, techniques, and instruments, pushing the boundaries of what was possible in music. They were also masters of delegation, knowing when to rely on each other's strengths and expertise.

Statistics show that the Beatles have sold more than 800 million records worldwide, making them one of the best-selling music artists of all time. They have also won numerous awards, including seven Grammy Awards and 15 Ivor Novello Awards.

Research also shows that the Beatles were heavily influenced by artists like Elvis Presley, Chuck Berry, and Little Richard. But they also drew inspiration from their own experiences, writing songs about love, loss, and life.

What allowed the Beatles to grow in their careers was their belief in themselves and their vision. They were willing to take risks, challenge the status quo, and pursue their passions. Their story is a testament to the power of creativity, collaboration, and perseverance.

So, if you're an ambitious, busy, results-driven professional looking to optimize your time, achieve your goals, and improve your performance, take a page out of the Beatles' book. Be open-minded, strategic, collaborative, and always willing to learn and grow. And who knows, you might change the world too.

Gerald J. Leonard

My journey toward understanding the essence of innovation and collaboration was significantly shaped by the histories and legacies of some of the most distinguished figures in the world of classical music. At the heart of this revelation was Antonio Toscanini, a maestro whose name resonated across the oceans, notably through his role as the conductor of the NBC Orchestra. Esteemed not only for his tenure with the New York Philharmonic and the Metropolitan Opera but also as the musical director of La Scala in Milan, Toscanini's mastery extended beyond the cello to unparalleled heights in leadership and orchestral direction. His weekly radio and TV broadcasts made his name synonymous with musical excellence in American households.

The narrative took a more personal turn when Toscanini, facing the unexpected illness of his principal bassist, initiated a nationwide search for a successor, culminating in the selection of David Walters, a principal bassist of the Pittsburgh Symphony. Walters' tenure under Toscanini's baton, which lasted until the maestro's retirement in 1955, was a testament to the transformative power of exceptional leadership. Walters himself acknowledged this, noting the heightened alertness and sensitivity instilled in musicians by Toscanini's guidance.

My own path crossed with Walters' decades later, in 1985, during my studies in double bass, which eventually led me to a professional studies program under his mentorship. Working with Walters, I discovered parallels between his teaching philosophy and Toscanini's leadership approach—both were demanding yet deeply rewarding, pushing musicians to surpass their perceived limits. Below is a letter of recommendation David Walters wrote on my behalf as I completed my year of professional studies with him.

Productivity Smarts

> THE JUILLIARD SCHOOL
> LINCOLN CENTER
> NEW YORK, NEW YORK 10023
>
> 11/12/86
>
> To Whom It May Concern:
>
> Gerald Leonard is a Graduate Student in Double Bass and Ensemble in my Class. He is technically accomplished, musically mature, a sensitive and interesting young artist.
>
> I recommend him most heartily for any competitions, auditions, performing or faculty positions he may apply for.
>
> Sincerely,
>
> David Walter
> Double Bass Faculty: Juilliard, Manhattan Sch.

This experience illuminated for me the broader implications of leadership beyond the confines of music. Toscanini, through his vision, skill, and unwavering commitment, crafted a culture of excellence that transcended individual performances to forge a legacy of passionate and proficient artists. Similarly, I came to realize that the role of a leader in any organization is to be the architect of its culture, crafting an environment that encourages innovation, fosters collaboration, and inspires all members to contribute their best.

In essence, the lessons I learned from the maestros of music about leadership, teaching, and excellence have profoundly influenced my belief in the power of a leader to cultivate a symphonic company culture. Just as Toscanini and Walters inspired greatness in their musicians, leaders across all fields have the responsibility to envision, embody, and enact values that nurture creativity, loyalty, and unparalleled performance within their teams.

The Beatles' career is a textbook example of how collaboration and innovation can drive success, both creatively and commercially. Their journey from a local band in Liverpool to international icons is punctuated by instances where their collaborative efforts and innovative approaches significantly impacted their music and legacy.

1. **Songwriting Collaboration—Lennon-McCartney Partnership:** One of the most famous aspects of the Beatles was the songwriting partnership between John Lennon and Paul McCartney. This collaboration was pivotal in creating many of their greatest hits. For instance, "A Hard Day's Night" and "Help!" were penned during this partnership, showcasing their ability to blend McCartney's upbeat melodies with Lennon's more introspective lyrics. This collaboration wasn't just about writing songs together; it was about blending two distinct creative visions into a harmonious and innovative musical expression.
2. **Musical Experimentation and Innovation:** The Beatles were never content with sticking to a single musical style. They consistently pushed the boundaries of what was considered conventional in popular music. Albums like *Revolver* and *Sgt. Pepper's Lonely Hearts*

Club Band exemplify this. *Sgt. Pepper*, for instance, incorporated a vast array of instruments and sounds, including a sitar in "Within You Without You" and a full orchestra in "A Day in the Life." This innovative use of diverse instruments and recording techniques was revolutionary at the time and set new standards in music production.

3. **Collaboration with George Martin:** Often referred to as the "Fifth Beatle," producer George Martin played a crucial role in the Beatles' success. His classical music background and willingness to experiment with new studio techniques were instrumental in realizing the band's creative visions. For instance, Martin's suggestion to speed up the recording of "Please Please Me" contributed significantly to the song's energetic vibe, turning it into their first major hit.

4. **Embracing the Studio as an Instrument:** During their later years, the Beatles increasingly saw the recording studio as an instrument in its own right. This period saw them transition from a touring band to a studio-based group. Albums like *Rubber Soul* and *Abbey Road* are examples of their innovative use of multi-track recording, tape loops, and sound effects, which were groundbreaking at the time.

5. **Cultural and Social Influence:** The Beatles also innovated in how they engaged with the cultural and social movements of their time. Songs like "Revolution" and "All You Need Is Love" resonated with the youth of the 1960s, reflecting and influencing the era's social changes. Their ability to tap into the zeitgeist was not just a testament to their musical prowess but also their deep understanding of their audience.

6. **Individual Contributions and Growth:** Each member of the Beatles also brought unique skills and

influences to the group. George Harrison's interest in Indian music and culture influenced songs like "Norwegian Wood," which featured a sitar. Ringo Starr's steady and creative drumming was the backbone of their sound. Their individual growth as musicians and songwriters also contributed to the band's collective evolution.

The Beatles' career is a textbook example of how collaboration and innovation can drive success, both creatively and commercially.

The Beatles' productivity superpower of collaboration and innovation is crucial for professionals to learn because it embodies the essence of successful teamwork and creative problem-solving. In today's complex work environments, where diverse skill sets and perspectives are essential, the ability to collaborate fosters a dynamic synergy that leads to innovative solutions. Learning from the Beatles teaches professionals to value each team member's strengths, embrace creativity, and navigate challenges collectively, ultimately driving success in their projects and endeavors.

Team Dynamics: Psychological studies emphasize the importance of positive team dynamics, trust, and effective communication. The Beatles' success underscores how a harmonious group dynamic fosters creativity and productivity.

Neural Synchronization: Neuroscientific research suggests that when people collaborate closely, their brain activity synchronizes. The close-knit collaboration within the Beatles likely led to neural synchronization, enhancing their collective creativity.

Innovation Culture: Business insights emphasize the need for an innovation culture that encourages risk-taking and experimentation. The Beatles' willingness to push boundaries and try new things exemplifies how cultivating an innovative culture leads to groundbreaking outcomes.

How does the diversity of perspectives within your team contribute to the collaborative process?

Are there mechanisms in place to ensure open communication and idea-sharing among team members?

How do you handle conflicts within the team to maintain a collaborative environment?

How is risk-taking encouraged, and what mechanisms exist for learning from both successes and failures?

How are team members empowered to take ownership of their ideas and contribute meaningfully to innovation?

Are there mechanisms for recognizing and celebrating individual and team contributions to innovation?

How do you balance the use of technology with maintaining a human-centric approach to collaboration?

How does your organization learn from both successful and unsuccessful collaborative endeavors?

What mechanisms exist for adapting strategies based on the feedback and insights gained through collaboration?

In what ways do you foster a continuous learning mindset within your team to drive innovation?

Incorporating the principles of collaboration and innovation, inspired by the Beatles, into project management can enhance team dynamics and project outcomes. Here are practical steps to achieve this:

1. **Foster a Collaborative Environment:**
    - Encourage open communication among team members.
    - Organize regular brainstorming sessions where all ideas are welcomed and considered.
    - Promote a culture of trust and respect where team members feel comfortable sharing their thoughts and feedback.
2. **Blend Diverse Skills and Perspectives:**
    - Assemble a team with a diverse set of skills and experiences, akin to how each Beatle brought a unique element to the band.
    - Encourage team members to contribute from their areas of strength, just as Lennon and McCartney combined their songwriting talents.
3. **Embrace and Encourage Innovation:**
    - Encourage team members to think outside the box and challenge the status quo.

- Allocate time and resources for experimentation and exploration of new ideas.
- Reward innovative thinking, even if it doesn't always lead to immediate success.

4. **Adopt Agile Methodologies:**
   - Implement an agile approach to project management, which emphasizes flexibility, continuous improvement, and rapid response to change.
   - Break projects into smaller, manageable parts, allowing for iterative development and frequent reassessment.

5. **Use Technology and Tools Creatively:**
   - Utilize project management tools and technologies creatively to enhance collaboration and efficiency.
   - Explore new software and digital platforms that can improve team communication and workflow.

6. **Encourage Individual Growth and Learning:**
   - Support team members in pursuing their personal and professional development goals.
   - Provide opportunities for learning new skills and cross-training within the team.

7. **Promote a Culture of Continuous Improvement:**
   - Regularly review and assess project processes and outcomes, always looking for ways to improve.
   - Encourage team members to provide feedback on what's working and what can be improved.

8. **Stay Adaptable to Change:**
   - Be prepared to pivot strategies when necessary, staying responsive to new information and changing circumstances.
   - Encourage flexibility and resilience within the team, just as the Beatles adapted their music and style over time.

9. **Celebrate Successes and Learn from Failures:**
   - Recognize and celebrate the team's achievements, big or small.
   - Treat failures as learning opportunities, reflecting on what went wrong and how to improve in the future.
10. **Connect Work to a Larger Purpose:**
    - Help team members see the bigger picture and understand how their work contributes to broader organizational goals.
    - Foster a sense of shared mission and purpose, much like the Beatles' shared vision for their music.

To further embed the principles of collaboration and innovation in project management, inspired by the Beatles, here are step-by-step exercises that teams can undertake:

Exercise 1: Collaborative Brainstorming Session

Objective: To generate a wide range of ideas and encourage creative thinking.

1. **Preparation:**
   - Choose a topic or problem that needs addressing.
   - Set up a comfortable meeting space, virtual or physical, where everyone can contribute.
2. **Idea Generation:**
   - Start with a brief overview of the topic.
   - Allow each team member to share their ideas without interruption or criticism.
3. **Idea Expansion:**
   - Encourage team members to build upon or combine ideas presented by others.
   - Use techniques like mind mapping to visually explore the connections between ideas.
4. **Consolidation:**
   - Group similar ideas and identify themes.

- Vote or discuss to narrow down to the most promising ideas.
5. **Action Plan:**
   - Assign tasks or further research to explore the selected ideas.
   - Schedule a follow-up meeting to assess progress.

Exercise 2: Skill-Sharing Workshop

Objective: To leverage the diverse skills within the team and foster a culture of continuous learning.

1. **Planning:**
   - Identify the unique skills and knowledge areas of team members.
   - Schedule a series of short workshops where each member can teach something to others.
2. **Conducting Workshops:**
   - Allocate a specific time for each workshop.
   - Encourage an interactive format with hands-on activities or demonstrations.
3. **Feedback and Application:**
   - After each workshop, discuss how these new skills can be applied to current or future projects.
   - Provide feedback to the presenter for improvement.

Exercise 3: Innovation Challenge

Objective: To stimulate innovative thinking and problem-solving.

1. **Set the Challenge:**
   - Present a real-world problem or a hypothetical scenario that requires a creative solution.
   - Define any constraints or guidelines for the solutions.
2. **Team Formation:**

- Divide the team into small groups, ensuring a mix of different skills in each group.
3. **Idea Development:**
    - Give teams a set amount of time to develop their solution.
    - Encourage the use of diverse brainstorming and problem-solving techniques.
4. **Presentation:**
    - Have each team present their solution to the group.
    - Include visual aids or prototypes if possible.
5. **Evaluation and Reflection:**
    - Discuss the strengths and weaknesses of each solution.
    - Reflect on the process and what was learned.

Exercise 4: Adaptability Role-Play
Objective: To improve adaptability and response to change.

1. **Scenario Setup:**
    - Create a scenario where an unexpected change affects a project (e.g., a sudden change in client requirements).
2. **Role-Playing:**
    - Assign team members different roles within the scenario.
    - Act out the scenario, allowing team members to respond to the change.
3. **Discussion:**
    - After the role-play, discuss the different approaches and reactions to the change.
    - Talk about what worked well and what could be improved.
4. **Learning Points:**

Productivity Smarts

- Summarize key takeaways on how to effectively manage change.

These exercises are designed to be practical and interactive, helping teams embrace the principles of collaboration and innovation in a tangible and engaging way. By regularly incorporating such activities, teams can develop the skills and mindset necessary to thrive in a dynamic and creative work environment.

Want to unlock the habits that fuel success? Get exclusive insights each week:

Chapter 6
Ed Sheeran

His productivity superpower was his ability to write songs quickly, with over 300 songs written in just three years.

"Write every day. Something will be bad, but it helps you get to the good stuff." —Ed Sheeran.

In the quaint town of Framlingham, nestled in the picturesque landscape of Suffolk, a young troubadour named Ed Sheeran was quietly sketching the blueprint for a musical revolution. Born in 1991, Ed would become synonymous not just with a soul-stirring voice but with a songwriting prowess that defied convention. His narrative unfolded against the backdrop of cobblestone streets, resonating with the echoes of melodies yet to be born.

Ed's musical journey commenced at a remarkably young age, fueled by an innate inclination for storytelling through the medium of song. Armed with a guitar, his constant companion, and a fervent passion for expression, he embarked on a mission that would reshape the contours of the music industry. His early years in Framlingham became the crucible for an artistic evolution that would transcend the ordinary.

The turning point in Ed's career arrived when he decided to make the leap to London, the pulsating heart of the music scene. In the vibrant chaos of the city, where dreams were both nurtured and tested, Ed found himself in a small flat with aspirations as vast as the sky. It was in this urban cocoon that his unique gift began to unravel—a gift that would set him on a trajectory of prolific songwriting at an unparalleled pace.

Ed's "aha" moment materialized in the realization that the key to success lay not only in the quality of his compositions but in the sheer quantity he could produce. The bustling energy of London fueled his creativity, and he embraced the discipline of consistent writing. A notebook and a guitar became his tools of choice, transforming mundane moments into lyrical gems.

The transformation of Ed Sheeran into a songwriting phenomenon was nothing short of extraordinary. Over a brief span from 2008 to 2011, he authored over 300 songs—a staggering testament to his ability to translate the tapestry of human emotions into verses and choruses. His songwriting process once shrouded in the simplicity of a notebook, was an alchemy that turned everyday experiences into lyrical masterpieces.

At the core of Ed's prolific output was an unwavering work ethic. Rather than waiting for inspiration to strike, he embraced the idea that creativity could be summoned through discipline. Each song became a snapshot of his journey, a reflection of life, love, heartbreak, and the intricate nuances of human existence.

Ed's journey to success unfolded not only through sheer numbers but also through the diversity of topics he explored. From tender ballads that tugged at heartstrings to upbeat anthems that reverberated with joy, his versatility knew no bounds. His lyrics, an intimate conversation with listeners, became a testament to the universality of human experiences.

The breakthrough arrived with Ed's debut album, +, which catapulted him into the global spotlight. Hits like "The A-Team" and "Lego House" showcased his ability to craft songs that resonated deeply with millions. His lyrical prowess transcended boundaries, bridging the gap between artist and audience.

Beyond the charts and accolades, Ed Sheeran's story serves as an inspiration to aspiring songwriters. His ability to write with such speed and authenticity underscores the notion that creativity is not a finite resource but a journey—a constant exploration. Every moment, no matter how mundane, can be a source of inspiration waiting to be woven into the fabric of a song.

Ed Sheeran's prolific songwriting journey exemplifies the transformative power of dedication, discipline, and an unbridled passion for one's craft. His ability to churn out over 300 songs in three years stands as a testament to the alchemy of relentless creativity. Aspiring artists can glean from Ed's story the importance of perseverance and the idea that sometimes, the most extraordinary creations emerge from a steadfast commitment to the art of songwriting.

I've come to understand that being prolific isn't just about output; it's about managing your most crucial asset—your energy. Today, I want to share insights on how energy management has become the cornerstone of my productivity and success and how you, too, can harness its power to become more prolific in your endeavors.

Energy management, in essence, is the strategic allocation and conservation of your energy resources to optimize performance across all areas of life. This approach transcends the conventional wisdom of time management, providing a more holistic and effective framework for achieving peak productivity. Through my journey, I've discovered that the key to being prolific lies not in stretching our days to work longer hours but in working smarter by managing our energy more effectively.

The realization dawned on me during a particularly challenging period when I was juggling multiple projects with tight deadlines. Despite my best efforts to manage my time, I found myself constantly drained, my creativity stifled by exhaustion. It was then that I stumbled upon the concept of energy management and its profound impact on productivity. Inspired by the works of experts like Tony Schwartz and the principles outlined in his book *The Power of Full Engagement*, I began to see productivity through a new lens.

I learned that our brains operate best in cycles of focus and rest, a concept supported by neuroscience research. This was a game-changer for me. I started to incorporate regular breaks into my schedule, prioritize sleep, and engage in activities that replenished my energy. These changes didn't just reduce my stress levels; they dramatically increased my output and the quality of my work. Projects that once seemed daunting now felt manageable, and my creative process flourished.

One of the myths I had to dispel was the notion that being prolific meant working relentlessly without pause. This couldn't be further from the truth. I discovered that by managing my energy, I could work more intensely and with greater focus during my peak periods and then fully disengage and recover during my downtime. This cycle of engagement and renewal became the foundation of my productivity strategy.

In project and portfolio management, this approach has been

invaluable. By viewing each project through the lens of energy management, I've been able to optimize my team's performance and achieve our goals with efficiency and less stress. We've become adept at breaking down tasks into manageable chunks, setting realistic daily objectives, and ensuring that everyone has the opportunity to recharge and maintain their energy levels.

To anyone looking to enhance their productivity and become more prolific, my advice is to start by assessing your energy patterns. Identify when you're most energetic and creative, and align your most challenging tasks with these peaks. Incorporate regular breaks to rest and recharge, prioritize activities that boost your energy, and don't underestimate the power of a good night's sleep.

Being prolific isn't about the quantity of work you produce but the quality and the sustainable energy behind it. By managing your energy effectively, you can unlock your full potential, reduce burnout, and achieve greater success in all your endeavors. Remember, in the quest to be prolific, your energy is your most precious resource. Manage it wisely.

"Don't wait for inspiration. It comes while one is working." —Henri Matisse

Being prolific in project management is about consistently delivering a high volume of quality work, a concept that transcends industries and finds relevance in the success stories of individuals like Ed Sheeran. Sheeran's career exemplifies how relentless creativity, discipline, and the ability to produce work at an exceptional pace can lead to monumental success. This principle is crucial in project management, where the ability to generate and execute a multitude of tasks, ideas, and solutions is key to driving projects forward and achieving objectives efficiently.

In project management, being prolific is not just about the sheer quantity of tasks completed but also about the strategic execution of these tasks to maintain quality and meet project goals. It involves a disciplined approach to work, where every task, no matter how small, is an opportunity for innovation and progress. This mirrors Sheeran's songwriting process, where he viewed every moment as a potential source of inspiration, turning the mundane into the extraordinary through disciplined creativity.

The concept of being prolific also encompasses the ability to work across various aspects of a project simultaneously, ensuring that progress is continuous and comprehensive. This requires a versatile skill set and an open-minded approach to problem-solving, much like how Sheeran explored diverse musical styles and themes in his work. For project managers, this means being adaptable and able to pivot between different project demands while maintaining a clear focus on the end goal.

Moreover, the essence of being prolific in project management is rooted in the ethos of perseverance. It's about pushing boundaries, constantly seeking improvement, and not being deterred by setbacks. Sheeran's journey from performing in small venues to achieving global fame underscores the importance of persistence and belief in one's work. Similarly, in project management, being prolific involves maintaining momentum through challenges, leveraging every setback as a learning opportunity, and staying committed to the project vision.

Being prolific is about embodying the principles of disciplined creativity, versatility, and persistence. It's about consistently delivering work that pushes the project forward, adapting to challenges with innovative solutions, and maintaining a steadfast commitment to achieving project objectives. This approach not only ensures project success but also fosters a culture of excellence and innovation within teams.

"Creativity doesn't wait for that perfect moment. It fashions its own perfect moments out of ordinary ones." —Bruce Garrabrandt

"Inspiration is for amateurs—the rest of us just show up and get to work." —Chuck Close

"Creativity is allowing yourself to make mistakes. Art is knowing which ones to keep." —Scott Adams

"The key to success is to start before you are ready." — Marie Forleo

"Don't wait for inspiration. It comes while one is working." —Henri Matisse

How do I maintain creativity while working quickly, and do I set aside time for experimentation in my work?

What habits or routines can I adopt to ensure I'm consistently producing, even on days when inspiration doesn't strike?

How can I refine my creative process to balance both speed and quality?

Do I allow myself the freedom to create imperfect work, knowing that it will lead to better results over time?

How do I avoid burnout when working at a fast pace, and what strategies can help me sustain energy and focus?

How do I push through creative blocks when working on long-term or fast-paced projects?

What lessons have I learned from quickly producing work, and how can I apply those lessons to future projects?

How do I handle criticism of work produced quickly, and how do I ensure that feedback contributes to my growth rather than holding me back?

How can I strike a balance between output and allowing time for reflection and revision?

In what ways can I encourage myself to produce more regularly and trust the process, even when the results aren't immediate?

Incorporating Ed Sheeran's Prolific Songwriting Approach into Project Management:

1. **Embrace Consistency and Discipline:**
   - **Action:** Encourage team members to adopt a consistent and disciplined approach to their tasks.
   - **Rationale:** Like Ed Sheeran's dedication to daily songwriting, consistent effort leads to a steady output, fostering productivity in project tasks.
2. **Encourage Frequent Idea Generation:**
   - **Action:** Promote a culture of brainstorming and idea generation within the team.
   - **Rationale:** Ed Sheeran's prolific songwriting was fueled by a constant flow of ideas. Similarly, frequent brainstorming sessions can lead to innovative solutions in project management.
3. **Document Ideas Promptly:**
   - **Action:** Implement a system for promptly documenting project ideas and insights.
   - **Rationale:** Ed Sheeran carried a notebook to capture ideas instantly. Similarly, project teams should document thoughts to prevent valuable insights from being lost.
4. **Cultivate a Collaborative Environment:**
   - **Action:** Foster collaboration and open communication among team members.
   - **Rationale:** Ed Sheeran often collaborated with others. In project management, a collaborative environment enhances creativity and allows for a diverse range of perspectives.
5. **Recognize the Value of Quantity and Quality:**
   - **Action:** Acknowledge that both quantity and quality are essential in project tasks.

- **Rationale:** Ed Sheeran's extensive song catalog showcases the importance of prolific output without compromising on quality. Similarly, project teams can strive for both quantity and excellence.
6. **Adopt Versatility in Approaches:**
    - **Action:** Encourage team members to be versatile in their problem-solving approaches.
    - **Rationale:** Ed Sheeran's diverse songwriting styles demonstrate the power of versatility. Project teams benefit from adaptability when faced with various challenges.
7. **Foster an Inclusive Creative Process:**
    - **Action:** Ensure that all team members feel included in the creative process.
    - **Rationale:** Ed Sheeran's collaborative nature extended to working with various artists. Similarly, inclusive project management allows diverse voices to contribute to solutions.
8. **Promote Continuous Improvement:**
    - **Action:** Establish a culture of continuous improvement within the team.
    - **Rationale:** Ed Sheeran's growth as a songwriter reflects the importance of constant improvement. In project management, teams should seek opportunities to enhance processes and outcomes.
9. **Celebrate Milestones and Achievements:**
    - **Action:** Recognize and celebrate project milestones and achievements.
    - **Rationale:** Ed Sheeran's success was marked by recognition and awards. Similarly, acknowledging project milestones boosts morale and motivates teams.
10. **Encourage Reflection and Adaptation:**

- **Action:** Promote reflection on project processes and outcomes and encourage adaptation based on lessons learned.
- **Rationale:** Ed Sheeran's evolution as an artist involved reflection and adaptation. In project management, continuous improvement comes from learning and adapting to changing circumstances.

By incorporating these practical steps inspired by Ed Sheeran's songwriting approach, project managers can foster a creative, collaborative, and prolific environment that contributes to the success of their projects.

1. **Daily Idea Sprint:**
   - **Objective:** Cultivate a habit of daily idea generation.
   - **Exercise:** Set aside 10 minutes each day for a rapid idea sprint. Team members jot down as many project-related ideas as possible. Share and discuss the most intriguing ones afterward.
2. **Digital Idea Hub Creation:**
   - **Objective:** Establish a centralized digital platform for idea sharing.
   - **Exercise:** Introduce a collaborative tool (e.g., online board or shared document) where team members can swiftly document and share project ideas. Encourage regular contributions.
3. **Cross-Functional Jam Session:**
   - **Objective:** Promote cross-functional collaboration.
   - **Exercise:** Periodically organize a cross-functional brainstorming session. Bring together members from different departments to tackle a project challenge collectively.
4. **Rapid Prototyping Workshop:**
   - **Objective:** Embrace a swift prototyping mindset.
   - **Exercise:** Choose a small project component and challenge teams to create rapid prototypes within a limited time frame. Evaluate the prototypes for innovation and practicality.
5. **Innovation Boost Workshops:**
   - **Objective:** Stimulate creative thinking.
   - **Exercise:** Conduct periodic innovation workshops where team members engage in activities designed to spark creativity. Encourage unconventional approaches to problem-solving.
6. **Open-Mindedness Training:**
   - **Objective:** Foster an open-minded culture.

- **Exercise:** Facilitate a workshop on open-mindedness, emphasizing its importance in project management. Encourage participants to share experiences where an open-minded approach led to success.
7. **Recognition Challenge:**
    - **Objective:** Acknowledge both quantity and quality.
    - **Exercise:** Introduce a recognition challenge where team members nominate peers for outstanding contributions, considering both the volume and excellence of completed tasks.
8. **Cross-Team Collaboration Event:**
    - **Objective:** Strengthen collaboration across teams.
    - **Exercise:** Organize a cross-team collaboration event or competition. Teams collaborate on a specific project task, emphasizing the benefits of diverse perspectives.
9. **Skill Enhancement Sessions:**
    - **Objective:** Promote continuous learning.
    - **Exercise:** Regularly schedule skill enhancement sessions where team members learn new tools, techniques, or approaches relevant to project management.
10. **Adaptation Through Retrospectives:**
    - **Objective:** Encourage reflection and adaptation.
    - **Exercise:** After completing a project milestone, conduct a retrospective meeting. Encourage team members to share insights, challenges, and suggestions for improvement.

By implementing these step-by-step exercises, project managers can infuse Ed Sheeran's productive mindset into their teams, fostering creativity, collaboration, and adaptability in project

Part Three

Pillar Three – Experimentation and Resilience

The Courage to Create and the Strength to Endure

Innovation is born from experimentation, and growth is sustained by resilience. Together, these forces drive progress in any field, empowering individuals and teams to push boundaries, embrace challenges, and overcome setbacks. Experimentation is the willingness to venture into the unknown, to try new approaches, and to challenge existing norms. It requires creativity, curiosity, and, most importantly, courage. Resilience, on the other hand, is the strength to persist through failure, adapt to unforeseen challenges, and continue striving for excellence. Without experimentation, progress stalls. Without resilience, progress falters.

This pillar, rooted in the legacies of Frank Zappa, Jimi Hendrix, and John Coltrane, demonstrates the powerful synergy between these two principles. These legendary artists didn't just create music —they redefined it. Their relentless experimentation and unyielding resilience enabled them to transcend conventions, innovate in ways that reshaped their industries, and leave behind enduring legacies. Their stories offer profound lessons for the modern workplace, where creativity and endurance are essential for navigating an ever-evolving landscape.

Frank Zappa epitomized the power of experimentation. Fearless in his approach, Zappa defied genre boundaries, blending rock, jazz, classical, and avant-garde music into a style entirely his own. He didn't just follow trends; he created them, challenging norms and inviting listeners to rethink what music could be. Zappa's fearlessness in the face of risk serves as a reminder that breakthroughs come from stepping outside the box. In the workplace, his legacy encourages leaders and teams to take calculated risks, embrace unconventional ideas, and explore new possibilities. Experimentation doesn't mean reckless abandon—it means creating a culture where bold ideas are nurtured and where failure is seen as a stepping stone rather than an endpoint.

Jimi Hendrix pushed the boundaries of his craft with groundbreaking guitar techniques and an unconventional approach to music. Hendrix's ability to think outside the box redefined how the guitar was played, making it an instrument of infinite possibilities. He didn't just master his tools; he reinvented their use, transforming limitations into opportunities. Hendrix's legacy teaches us to approach problems with fresh perspectives, challenging norms, and breaking through traditional constraints. In the workplace, this means fostering an environment where innovation thrives, where old problems are met with new solutions, and where teams are empowered to question the status quo.

John Coltrane adds another dimension to this pillar with his unparalleled resilience and dedication to mastery. Coltrane's relentless pursuit of technical and spiritual growth was driven by an unshakable belief in the power of music to transcend the ordinary. His ability to persevere through challenges and continue refining his craft serves as a model for building resilience in the face of adversity. Coltrane reminds us that resilience isn't just about enduring hardship

—it's about growing stronger because of it. In the workplace, resilience is the foundation that allows teams to learn from failure, adapt to change, and maintain momentum in even the most challenging environments.

Experimentation and resilience are deeply interconnected. Experimentation sparks innovation, but resilience sustains it, allowing teams and individuals to navigate the inevitable setbacks that come with trying something new. Together, they create a cycle of growth: experimentation leads to discovery, resilience ensures persistence, and the lessons learned fuel further experimentation.

As you reflect on this pillar, consider how these principles apply to your professional context. Are you creating opportunities for experimentation within your team? Are you encouraging calculated risks and supporting creative problem-solving? Are you cultivating resilience, ensuring that challenges and setbacks are met with adaptability and determination? These questions are crucial for building a culture that thrives on innovation and sustains progress over time.

In the chapters ahead, we'll explore how to integrate these lessons into your work. From fostering a culture of experimentation inspired by Zappa and Hendrix to building the resilience modeled by Coltrane, you'll gain actionable insights into how to turn challenges into opportunities and ideas into breakthroughs. Whether you're leading a team, managing a project, or navigating personal growth, this pillar will provide the tools to think boldly, adapt courageously, and persevere unwaveringly.

Experimentation and resilience are not just about achieving success—they're about redefining what success means. With inspiration from Zappa, Hendrix, and Coltrane, you'll discover how to create, innovate, and endure in ways that leave a lasting impact.

Chapter 7
Frank Zappa

"Pushing the boundaries is not just about breaking through limits; it's about redefining what's possible." —Unknown

Frank Zappa's life and career present a compelling narrative for business professionals, illustrating the profound impact of creativity, hard work, and individuality in achieving success. Born in 1940 in Baltimore, Maryland, Zappa grew up in an unconventional household. With a chemist father and a librarian mother, his home was one where intellect and curiosity were nurtured. This upbringing played a significant role in shaping his distinctive approach to music and life.

From a young age, Zappa was captivated by the avant-garde compositions of Edgard Varèse and Igor Stravinsky, and he began experimenting with his own musical creations as a teenager. This early exposure to diverse musical genres laid the foundation for his eclectic and innovative style. In the business world, this parallels the importance of a broad knowledge base and an openness to diverse influences for fostering innovation.

Despite his unique upbringing and talents, Zappa's journey was not without challenges. He was a nonconformist in an industry that often favored convention, and his outspoken views on political and social issues frequently put him at odds with the mainstream music industry. He faced censorship, legal battles, and criticism for his controversial lyrics and album artwork. Yet, like a resilient entrepreneur, Zappa remained unwavering in his commitment to his vision and craft.

Zappa's "aha" moment came when he realized that his music could serve as a powerful platform for his ideas and beliefs. Embracing his outsider status, he used his art to challenge societal norms and the status quo, much like a disruptive innovator in the business world.

His transformation into a prolific musician and composer was nothing short of remarkable. Over his career, Zappa released over 60 albums, selling over 40 million copies worldwide, weaving a tapestry of sound that spanned multiple genres, from jazz to rock to hip-hop. His induction into the Rock and Roll Hall of Fame in 1995 was a testament to his lasting impact on the music industry.

One of Zappa's most notable strengths was his relentless drive to push the boundaries of his art. He never settled for the ordinary and constantly sought new ways to innovate and experiment. This unyielding pursuit of innovation parallels the mindset needed in business to stay ahead in competitive and ever-changing markets.

A key aspect of his influence is his role as a producer and his mastery of the recording studio. His innovative techniques in the studio and his insistence on high-quality recording standards demonstrate a commitment to excellence and attention to detail that is crucial in any business endeavor. Zappa's approach to production, where he was involved in every aspect of the process, mirrors a hands-on leadership style in business, ensuring quality and consistency in every product.

Zappa's interaction with his band members offers another valuable lesson for business. He was known for his demanding leadership style, expecting high levels of professionalism and technical proficiency. This aspect of his narrative emphasizes the importance of setting high standards and fostering a culture of excellence within an organization.

Moreover, Zappa's influences were as varied as his musical output. From classical composers like Stravinsky and Varèse to jazz legends Charlie Parker and Miles Davis and the blues and R&B of his youth, he absorbed a spectrum of sounds and styles. This eclectic influence can be likened to successful businesses that draw upon a wide range of sources for inspiration and innovation.

Zappa's beliefs were integral to his success. His advocacy for creative expression, individuality, and personal freedom, as well as his willingness to challenge authority and convention, are qualities that can be transformative in the business environment. His story is a powerful reminder of the impact that creativity, hard work, and a commitment to one's vision can have.

During an insightful interview, I had the privilege of engaging with Beverly Jones, a remarkable individual whose story is a testament to the power of pushing the envelope in her relentless pursuit of equity in the professional realm. Her journey, marked by significant challenges and groundbreaking achievements, offered profound lessons on pushing limits and innovating within traditionally restrictive environments.

From her early days as an undergraduate, she was acutely aware of the systemic barriers that stifled opportunities for women and minorities in academia and the workforce. Faced with a societal expectation that limited women to roles that were dismissively categorized under "women's pages," her aspirations extended far beyond. Her refusal to be pigeonholed into such narrow confines sparked a determination to not only carve out her path but also to pave the way for others to follow.

Her narrative unfolded, revealing a transition from campus activism to a pioneering role at Ohio University, where she spearheaded efforts to implement Title IX. This endeavor wasn't just a job; it was a mission to dismantle the institutional barriers that hindered equitable access to education and employment opportunities for all, regardless of gender or race.

Her journey didn't stop there. She ventured into law, bringing her advocacy to the corridors of power where decisions were made and policies were crafted. Each step of her career, from legal practice to executive roles, was underpinned by a deep-seated passion for justice and inclusivity. This passion was not merely a guiding principle but a driving force that propelled her to challenge and redefine the status quo at every turn.

This interview wasn't just a recounting of past triumphs; it was a reflection on the enduring need for vigilance and advocacy in the pursuit of equity and diversity in the workplace. Her story is a powerful reminder that the fight for equality is ongoing, requiring each of us to contribute to the creation of a more inclusive and equitable professional landscape.

Through her experiences, she imparted invaluable insights into the essence of innovation and collaboration, emphasizing that true progress is only achievable when diverse voices are heard and varied perspectives are valued. Her journey illustrates that pushing the limits is not just about individual perseverance but about collective action and the shared responsibility to foster environments where everyone has the opportunity to thrive.

The remarkable journey of the individual in this interview is a vivid illustration of how pushing boundaries and fostering innovation are critical in project management as much as they are in advocacy and legal reform. Her path from confronting systemic barriers in academia and the workforce to spearheading the implementation of Title IX embodies the essence of project management: identifying challenges, devising strategic plans, and executing actions that lead to significant, transformative outcomes.

In project management, as in her advocacy, the ability to envision a better future and systematically work toward it despite the hurdles is paramount. Her unwavering determination not to be confined by societal expectations and her strategic approach to dismantling institutional barriers mirror the project manager's role in navigating obstacles, marshaling resources, and steering projects to successful completion.

Her transition into law and executive roles further underscores the importance of adaptability and strategic thinking in project management. Each step of her career was marked by a clear vision and a meticulously planned approach to achieving her goals. This strategic mindset is akin to the project manager's task of planning, executing, and closing projects, ensuring that each step aligns with the overarching objectives while remaining agile enough to adapt to unforeseen challenges.

Moreover, her emphasis on the value of diverse voices and perspectives in achieving true progress highlights a crucial aspect of project management: collaboration. Just as her advocacy work benefited from the collective action and shared responsibility of those committed to fostering inclusive environments, successful project management relies on the collaborative efforts of cross-functional teams, each bringing unique insights and expertise to the table.

Gerald J. Leonard

Her narrative also serves as a reminder of the continuous need for innovation in project management practices. Just as she constantly sought new ways to advocate for equity and diversity, project managers must continually seek innovative solutions and methodologies to improve project outcomes and efficiency. The pursuit of innovation in project management not only enhances the effectiveness of individual projects but also contributes to the evolution of the field as a whole.

In sharing her story, she not only sheds light on the persistent challenges but also celebrates the progress made toward a more inclusive future. Her journey is a powerful testament to the impact that dedication, strategic planning, and a commitment to innovation can have, offering valuable lessons for project managers and professionals in all fields. Her narrative encourages us to push the limits, embrace innovation, and work collaboratively toward our goals, reminding us of the transformative power of determined action and strategic vision in project management and beyond.

One of Zappa's most notable strengths was his relentless drive to push the boundaries of his art.

Frank Zappa's productivity superpower, characterized by his relentless drive to innovate and experiment, is crucial for professionals to learn because it embodies the spirit of creativity, adaptability, and continuous improvement. In today's fast-paced and ever-changing work environments, professionals need to be able to think outside the box, challenge conventional wisdom, and embrace new ideas in order to stay ahead of the curve. By adopting Zappa's approach to productivity, professionals can cultivate a mindset of innovation, resilience, and growth, allowing them to thrive in the face of challenges and drive meaningful change within their organizations.

Psychology, neuroscience, and business research **to push the boundaries of his art constantly.**

Frank Zappa's approach to pushing the boundaries of his art was deeply rooted in psychology, neuroscience, and business principles. He understood the importance of tapping into the human psyche to create music that resonated with his audience on a profound level. Zappa's keen insight into human behavior allowed him to experiment with unconventional sounds and themes, pushing the boundaries of what was considered acceptable in music.

From a neuroscience perspective, Zappa was fascinated by the brain's capacity for creativity and innovation. He recognized that by exploring new musical territories and challenging established norms, he could stimulate neural pathways and evoke powerful emotional responses in listeners. This understanding of the brain's plasticity and adaptability fueled his relentless pursuit of new ideas and sounds.

In terms of business, Zappa was a savvy entrepreneur who understood the importance of innovation and differentiation in a competitive market. He recognized that in order to stand out from the crowd, he needed to constantly push the boundaries of his art and offer something unique to his audience. By embracing risk-taking and experimentation, Zappa was able to carve out a niche for himself in the music industry and build a loyal fan base that appreciated his bold and unconventional approach.

Overall, Frank Zappa's ability to push the boundaries of his art was informed by a deep understanding of psychology, neuroscience, and business principles. His willingness to explore new ideas and challenge established norms not only revolutionized the world of music but also served as a valuable lesson for professionals in any field looking to drive innovation and achieve success.

What does it mean to "push the boundaries" in your own field or area of interest?

How comfortable are you with stepping outside of your comfort zone to explore new ideas or approaches?

What are some examples of individuals or organizations that have successfully pushed the boundaries in their respective fields? What can we learn from their experiences?

What are the potential risks and rewards associated with pushing the boundaries? How do you weigh these factors in your decision-making process?

What obstacles or barriers might prevent you from pushing the boundaries in your work or personal life, and how can you overcome them?

How do you balance the desire to innovate and experiment with the need to maintain stability and consistency?

How can pushing the boundaries contribute to personal growth and development?

How do you cultivate a mindset that embraces experimentation and risk-taking?

What role does collaboration play in pushing the boundaries? How can working with others enhance your ability to innovate?

In what ways can you apply the lessons learned from individuals like Frank Zappa to your own efforts to push the boundaries and drive meaningful change?

Incorporating the principles exemplified by Frank Zappa's career into project management can lead to enhanced innovation, adaptability, and a strong commitment to quality in any business setting. Here are practical steps to achieve this:

1. **Cultivate a Culture of Creativity and Openness:**
   - Encourage team members to express their unique ideas and perspectives, just as Zappa embraced diverse musical influences.
   - Create a safe space for brainstorming where unconventional ideas are welcomed and valued.
2. **Promote Cross-Disciplinary Learning:**
   - Like Zappa's eclectic musical education, encourage team members to explore knowledge and skills outside their expertise.
   - Facilitate cross-departmental collaborations or workshops to broaden the team's perspective and skillset.
3. **Foster an Environment for Experimentation:**
   - Allocate time and resources for team members to experiment with new methods, technologies, or processes.
   - Encourage a trial-and-error approach, understanding

that not every experiment leads to immediate success but can be a learning opportunity.

4. **Encourage Challenging the Status Quo:**
   o Motivate the team to question existing processes and think about how they can be improved or innovated.
   o Reward initiative and courage in proposing new ways of doing things, even if it goes against traditional practices.

5. **Focus on Quality and Attention to Detail:**
   o Emphasize the importance of quality and precision in every aspect of the project, mirroring Zappa's meticulous approach in the studio
   o Implement regular quality checks and encourage team members to take ownership of their work.

6. **Resilience in Facing Challenges:**
   o Prepare the team to handle setbacks and obstacles, using Zappa's career challenges as an example of resilience.
   o Conduct scenario planning or resilience training to help team members navigate through difficult periods.

7. **Advocate for Artistic Freedom and Individuality:**
   o Recognize and celebrate the individual strengths and styles of each team member.
   o Allow for personal expression within the project framework, which can lead to innovative solutions and a more engaged team.

8. **Implement Rigorous a Work Ethic:**
   o Encourage a strong work ethic, focusing on dedication and commitment to project goals.
   o Set clear expectations and lead by example, illustrating the importance of hard work and dedication.

9. **Encourage Continuous Learning and Improvement:**
    - Foster a culture of continuous learning, where team members are encouraged to enhance their skills and knowledge.
    - Regularly review project processes and outcomes, seeking opportunities for improvement and growth.
10. **Promote Diversity of Thought:**
    - Actively seek and include diverse perspectives in decision-making and problem-solving.
    - Encourage team members to draw inspiration from a wide range of sources, much like Zappa's diverse musical influences.

By implementing these steps, project managers can create a dynamic and innovative work environment that values creativity, encourages experimentation, and maintains a high standard of quality and detail, much like Frank Zappa's approach to his music and career.

Incorporating the principles inspired by Frank Zappa's approach to music and creativity into project management can be facilitated through specific exercises. These exercises aim to foster a culture of innovation, adaptability, and meticulous attention to detail within a team.

Exercise 1: Creative Brainstorming Sessions

Objective: To encourage creative and unconventional thinking.

1. **Theme Selection:**
    - Choose a broad theme related to a current project or challenge.
2. **Idea Generation:**

- Conduct a brainstorming session where team members are encouraged to think outside the box, proposing unconventional and innovative solutions.
3. **Idea Development:**
   - Select the most promising ideas and develop them further in smaller groups.
4. **Presentation and Feedback:**
   - Have each group present their ideas and receive feedback from the rest of the team.

Exercise 2: Cross-Disciplinary Learning Workshop
Objective: To broaden the team's perspective and skill set.

1. **Skill Sharing:**
   - Identify unique skills or knowledge areas within the team.
2. **Workshop Planning:**
   - Organize a series of short workshops where team members can teach something related to their skill or interest to others.
3. **Workshop Execution:**
   - Conduct the workshops, focusing on interactive and practical learning experiences.

Exercise 3: Challenge the Norm
Objective: To cultivate a mindset of questioning and innovating on existing processes.

1. **Identify a Standard Process:**
   - Choose a standard process or method currently used in the team.
2. **Critical Analysis:**
   - Individually or in groups, analyze the process and

identify areas for potential improvement or innovation.
3. **Alternative Proposal:**
   - Encourage teams to develop alternative approaches or improvements to the process.
4. **Discussion and Implementation:**
   - Discuss the proposed alternatives and plan to implement the most feasible ones.

Exercise 4: Quality Focus Group
Objective: To emphasize the importance of quality and attention to detail.

1. **Project Review:**
   - Select a recent project or work product of the team.
2. **Detail-Oriented Analysis:**
   - Review the project with a focus on quality and attention to detail.
3. **Improvement Plan:**
   - Identify areas for improvement and create a plan to enhance quality in future projects.

Exercise 5: Resilience Training
Objective: To build the team's resilience in facing challenges.

1. **Resilience Workshop:**
   - Conduct a workshop on resilience, discussing strategies to handle setbacks and stress.
2. **Role-Playing:**
   - Create scenarios where team members must navigate through challenging situations.
3. **Reflection and Discussion:**
   - Reflect on the role-play experiences and discuss resilience strategies.

By regularly incorporating these exercises into the team's routine, project managers can foster an environment that values creativity, embraces challenges, and maintains a high standard of quality, drawing inspiration from Frank Zappa's innovative and meticulous approach to his work.

Don't let burnout hold you back. Get expert advice on thriving under pressure here:

Chapter 8
Jimi Hendrix

His productivity superpower was his ability to think outside the box and come up with new ideas that no one else had thought of before.

"I found myself in too much of a box situation." —Jimi Hendrix

In the annals of musical history, Jimi Hendrix stands as a monumental figure, not just for his unparalleled skills as a guitarist

but also as a paragon of creativity, innovation, and resilience. His story is particularly resonant for busy corporate professionals seeking to optimize time and enhance performance.

Born in 1942 in Seattle into a low-income family, Hendrix's journey from humble beginnings to becoming one of the greatest guitarists of all time is a narrative of overcoming adversity and embracing individuality. Despite the financial constraints and racial discrimination he faced, Hendrix's passion for music was undeterred. His childhood, marked by hardships, fueled his drive to succeed against all odds.

Hendrix's road to stardom was fraught with challenges. The racism and discrimination he faced were stark realities of his time. In one instance, his race led to him being ousted from a band, a testament to the obstacles he had to navigate. Yet, these barriers only strengthened his resolve to carve out his own path in the music world.

Before his breakthrough, Hendrix played in various bands and worked as a session musician. These experiences were instrumental in shaping his unique style. It was during this time that he had his epiphanic moment—the realization that conforming to traditional music rules was not his path. Instead, he embraced his distinctiveness, weaving his unique style into the tapestry of his music.

This transformation was pivotal. Hendrix began to harness his creativity, thinking outside the box to produce sounds never heard before. His use of feedback and distortion, once considered unconventional, became his signature. This approach was not just a technique; it was an expression of his individuality, a manifestation of his refusal to fit into preconceived molds.

Hendrix's career, though tragically short, was meteoric. With The Jimi Hendrix Experience, he released three critically acclaimed albums, each a testament to his innovative spirit. His headline performance at Woodstock in 1969 remains one of the most iconic moments in music history. In 1992, his genius was further recognized with an induction into the Rock and Roll Hall of Fame.

More than his music, Hendrix was a trailblazer who redefined what it meant to be a musician. His belief in embracing individuality and creativity has inspired a multitude of artists across various genres. He showed that true innovation often comes from thinking outside the box and daring to be different.

Hendrix's influences were eclectic, ranging from blues legends like Muddy Waters and B.B. King to non-musical inspirations like science fiction and the counterculture movement of the 1960s. This wide array of influences further fueled his creative genius, allowing him to blend different elements into his music.

For the busy corporate professional, Jimi Hendrix's story is a beacon of inspiration. It teaches the value of embracing one's unique talents and perspectives. It highlights that creativity and innovation are not just about breaking the rules but about seeing beyond them. Hendrix's legacy shows that by thinking differently and tapping into our inherent creativity, we can achieve extraordinary success.

So, take a page out of Hendrix's book. Embrace your individuality, foster your creativity, and don't be afraid to venture off the beaten path. Who knows what heights of success this might lead you to in your professional journey?

Reflecting on the essence of innovation in project management, I'm drawn to the countless moments where thinking outside the box not only saved projects from the brink of failure but also propelled them into realms of success previously unimaginable. These experiences, woven into the very fabric of my career, underscore a fundamental truth: the power of new ideas cannot be overstated.

Consider the time when my team faced a seemingly insurmountable challenge. Traditional methods were failing, deadlines were looming, and morale was waning. It was a pivotal moment that demanded a radical departure from the norm. Encouraged to think freely, without the constraints of conventional wisdom, we embarked on a brainstorming journey that felt more like alchemy than process management. The result was a groundbreaking solution that not only solved our immediate problem but also redefined our approach to project challenges.

This epiphany was not a solitary event but a recurring theme. Time and again, I've witnessed the transformative power of novel ideas. Whether it was reimagining a workflow that enhanced efficiency beyond our wildest dreams or adopting a technology that was yet to become mainstream, the courage to venture into uncharted territory has been our compass.

The journey of innovation is fraught with risks and uncertainties. There were moments of doubt where the allure of the tried and true tempted us to retreat to the safety of familiar ground. Yet, it was in these moments of vulnerability that the most profound breakthroughs emerged. By embracing the unknown and viewing failure not as a setback but as a stepping stone, we cultivated a culture of relentless experimentation.

This culture of innovation has extended beyond the confines of individual projects. It has shaped my philosophy on leadership and teamwork. Encouraging team members to challenge assumptions and voice their wildest ideas without fear of judgment has unlocked a wellspring of creativity. It's a reminder that the most revolutionary ideas often come from the most unexpected places.

Moreover, the pursuit of new ideas has not been a solitary endeavor. It has fostered collaborations that span disciplines and industries, bringing together diverse minds united by a common goal: to innovate. These partnerships have been a testament to the fact that when we broaden our horizons, the potential for discovery is limitless.

In reflecting on these experiences, I am convinced more than ever that the future of project management—and indeed, of any endeavor —lies in our ability to think outside the box. It's a journey of constant learning, embracing change, and daring to imagine the impossible. As I look ahead, I am filled with anticipation for the new ideas that await, for the challenges they will solve, and for the horizons they will expand. In the realm of innovation, the only limit is our imagination.

Productivity Smarts

"Instead of thinking outside the box, get rid of the box."
—Deepak Chopra

In my journey through the corridors of corporate innovation and project management, the tale of Jimi Hendrix resonates deeply, not just as a testament to musical genius but as a parable of creativity and breaking the mold. His story, from a humble beginning in Seattle to becoming a guitar legend, echoes the trials and triumphs I've encountered in fostering innovation within the corporate realm. Hendrix's refusal to conform and explore sounds and techniques that were unheard of mirrors the ethos I've strived to instill in my teams: the courage to venture beyond the conventional and embrace the unique.

Reflecting on Hendrix's journey, I see parallels in the world of project management and productivity. His challenges, from overcoming racial discrimination to pushing the boundaries of music, underscore the universal struggle against limitations—both external and internal. In a corporate setting, these barriers often manifest as rigid processes, risk aversion, and a reluctance to challenge the status quo. Yet, it's in the face of these barriers that the potential for innovation is most potent.

Hendrix's epiphany, realizing that his path lay not in conforming but in embracing his individuality, sparked a transformation that revolutionized music. This lesson is invaluable for corporate professionals: Innovation is not merely about improving efficiencies or adopting new technologies. It's about seeing beyond the apparent, questioning why things are done a certain way, and daring to imagine how they could be done differently.

The process of innovation, much like Hendrix's use of feedback and distortion, often involves embracing what others might consider mistakes or flaws and turning them into strengths. In project management, this means fostering a culture where experimentation is encouraged and where failure is seen not as a setback but as a vital step on the path to discovery. It's about creating an environment where team members feel empowered to voice unconventional ideas, test new approaches, and learn from the outcomes, regardless of success or failure.

Moreover, Hendrix's story highlights the importance of drawing inspiration from a broad spectrum of sources. His influences ranged from blues and rock to science fiction and the social movements of his time. Similarly, in the pursuit of innovation, we must look beyond our immediate field, drawing inspiration from diverse disciplines, cultures, and even personal interests. This eclectic approach can lead to breakthrough ideas that might never emerge from a more narrow focus.

As I look to the future, inspired by Hendrix's legacy, I'm convinced that the key to unlocking the full potential of project management and productivity lies in our ability to think outside the box. It's about nurturing a mindset of constant improvement and experimentation, welcoming diverse perspectives, and challenging our own assumptions. In doing so, we not only pay homage to Hendrix's spirit of innovation but also pave the way for breakthroughs that, like his music, have the power to change the landscape forever.

So, as we navigate the complexities of the corporate world, let us remember the lessons of Jimi Hendrix. Let us embrace our individuality, foster our creativity, and never fear to venture off the beaten path. In the realm of project management and productivity, as in music, the most profound innovations often come from the courage to be different.

"If everyone is thinking alike, then somebody isn't thinking." — George S. Patton

Productivity Smarts

"I'm good at thinking outside the box, so much that you realize it's not a box to begin with." —will.i.am

How can embracing your individuality set you apart from others in your professional field?

What are some unique traits or skills you have that you may not be fully leveraging?

In what ways can fostering creativity lead to breakthroughs in your professional journey?

How can you cultivate an environment that encourages innovative thinking in your daily work?

What risks are involved in venturing off the beaten path, and how can you mitigate them while still thinking outside the box?

How do you balance creative exploration with practical business constraints?

How do unconventional approaches help you discover opportunities others may overlook?

Can you think of a recent challenge where thinking outside the box led to unexpected solutions?

What lessons can be learned from figures like Hendrix, who achieved success by breaking norms and defying expectations?

How can you apply those lessons to your own professional development?

What are the potential rewards of challenging traditional methods in your industry, and are you prepared to face the obstacles that may come with it?

How do you prepare yourself mentally and professionally for potential failure when experimenting with new ideas?

Drawing inspiration from the story of Jimi Hendrix, project managers can integrate his innovative spirit and creative mindset into their work. Here are practical steps to incorporate these elements into project management:

1. **Embrace Individuality Within the Team**

- **Recognize Unique Talents:** Identify and appreciate the unique skills and perspectives each team member

brings to the table, just as Hendrix embraced his distinct style.
- **Encourage Personal Contributions:** Allow team members to contribute in ways that leverage their individual strengths and experiences.

2. Foster a Culture of Creativity and Innovation

- **Brainstorming Sessions:** Regularly hold brainstorming sessions where unconventional ideas are welcomed and encouraged.
- **Creative Problem-Solving:** Challenge the team to find creative solutions to project obstacles, thinking beyond traditional methods.

3. Experiment with New Techniques and Tools

- **Explore New Tools:** Just as Hendrix experimented with feedback and distortion, try out new project management tools and technologies.
- **Pilot Projects:** Implement small-scale pilot projects to test new approaches or techniques before rolling them out on a larger scale.

4. Encourage Risk-Taking Within Safe Boundaries

- **Calculated Risks:** Promote taking calculated risks, ensuring that these ventures are within the project's risk tolerance.
- **Learn from Mistakes:** Create an environment where mistakes are viewed as learning opportunities.

5. Break Down Conventional Barriers

- **Question the Status Quo:** Regularly review and question existing project processes and norms and be open to redefining them.
- **Cross-functional collaboration:** Encourage collaboration across different departments or specialties to bring diverse perspectives to the project.

6. Promote Continuous Learning and Adaptation

- **Professional Development:** Encourage continuous learning and upskilling among team members.
- **Adaptability:** Foster a mindset of adaptability, where change is seen as an opportunity for growth and improvement.

7. Leverage Diverse Influences

- **Seek External Inspiration:** Draw inspiration from various fields and industries, not just those directly related to the project or business.
- **Diversity of Thought:** Encourage team members to bring insights from their personal interests and experiences into the project.

8. Prioritize Authenticity and Passion

- **Passion Projects:** Allow team members to work on aspects of the project they are passionate about.
- **Authentic Leadership:** Lead by example, showing genuine enthusiasm and commitment to the project.

9. Incorporate Feedback and Reflection

- **Regular Reviews:** Hold regular project review sessions to reflect on what is working and what can be improved.
- **Constructive Feedback:** Create an environment where constructive feedback is encouraged and valued.

10. Celebrate Creativity and Success

- **Recognize Innovations:** Acknowledge and celebrate when team members come up with innovative solutions or when a new approach proves successful.
- **Share Success Stories:** Share successes and innovative solutions with the wider organization to inspire others.

By integrating these steps, inspired by Jimi Hendrix's extraordinary approach to music, project managers can create a more dynamic, innovative, and successful project environment. This approach not only leads to improved project outcomes but also contributes to a more engaged and motivated team.

To infuse Jimi Hendrix's innovative spirit and creativity into project management, consider the following step-by-step exercises. These exercises are designed to encourage thinking outside the box, foster creativity, and enhance team collaboration.

Exercise 1: Creative Brainstorming Sessions
Objective: Generate innovative ideas and solutions.

- **Step 1:** Present a project-related challenge to the team.
- **Step 2:** Organize a brainstorming session where all ideas are welcomed, no matter how unconventional.
- **Step 3:** Encourage team members to build on each other's ideas.
- **Step 4:** Evaluate the ideas and select the most promising ones for further exploration.

Exercise 2: Role Reversal
Objective: Encourage empathy and new perspectives.

- **Step 1:** Pair team members with different roles or expertise.
- **Step 2:** Ask them to present a part of the project from their partner's perspective.
- **Step 3:** Discuss as a group what new insights or ideas emerged from this exercise.

Exercise 3: The "What If" Game
Objective: Promote creative problem-solving.

- **Step 1:** Present a current project scenario.
- **Step 2:** Ask the team, "What if we did it completely differently?"
- **Step 3:** Discuss the potential outcomes of this radical change.
- **Step 4:** Identify if any elements of this "different way" can be realistically integrated into the project.

Exercise 4: Creative Inspirations
Objective: Draw inspiration from unrelated fields.

- **Step 1:** Assign each team member to research a non-related field or subject.
- **Step 2:** Have them present how principles or ideas from that field could apply to the project.
- **Step 3:** Discuss as a team how these new insights can be incorporated into your work.

Exercise 5: Failure Analysis
Objective: Learn from mistakes and foster a risk-taking culture.

- **Step 1:** Reflect on a past project or decision that didn't go as planned.
- **Step 2:** Analyze what went wrong and why.
- **Step 3:** Discuss what could have been done differently and how this learning can be applied to current projects.

Exercise 6: Cross-Functional Collaboration Workshop
Objective: Encourage diverse thinking and collaboration.

- **Step 1:** Organize a workshop with members from different departments.
- **Step 2:** Present a common project challenge and ask for input from all areas.
- **Step 3:** Explore how these diverse perspectives can lead to more comprehensive solutions.

Exercise 7: Passion Project Time
Objective: Encourage individual creativity and innovation.

- **Step 1:** Allocate a certain amount of time for team members to work on a project-related subject they are passionate about.
- **Step 2:** At the end of this period, have them present their findings or creations.
- **Step 3:** Discuss how these passion projects can benefit the main project.

Exercise 8: Improvisation and Adaptability Challenge
Objective: Enhance adaptability and quick thinking.

- **Step 1:** Present an unexpected change in project conditions.

- **Step 2:** Challenge the team to come up with an immediate plan of action.
- **Step 3:** Evaluate the effectiveness and creativity of the responses.

By regularly engaging in these exercises, teams can develop a stronger sense of creativity, improve problem-solving skills, and enhance their ability to innovate, much like Jimi Hendrix revolutionized the world of music with his unique style and approach.

Learn how to create unstoppable teams with weekly leadership insights—sign up now:

Chapter 9
John Coltrane

C oltrane's productivity superpower was his dedication to constant improvement and experimentation.

"My music is the spiritual expression of what I am: my faith, my knowledge, my being" —John Coltrane

Gerald J. Leonard

John Coltrane's journey, rich in lessons of resilience, innovation, and spiritual depth, offers a compelling blueprint for ambitious professionals in any field. His story is not just about musical triumph but also about personal transformation and unwavering dedication to his art.

Born into a family where gospel music resonated through the household, Coltrane's early life in North Carolina was steeped in musical influences. His affinity for the saxophone emerged in high school, marking the beginning of a lifelong passion. His studies at the Ornstein School of Music were not merely academic; they were a deep dive into the technical intricacies of music, preparing him for the complex world of jazz.

Coltrane's career, though illustrious, was riddled with challenges. His struggle with drug addiction and the consequent professional setbacks, including being fired from Miles Davis' band, were significant hurdles. Yet, these adversities were the crucibles that forged his character. Coltrane's ability to turn these challenges into motivation for self-improvement mirrors the resilience required in any high-pressure career.

The year 1957 was a watershed moment for Coltrane. His spiritual awakening brought a seismic shift in his life and music. He emerged from his struggles with a renewed sense of purpose, channeling his spiritual energy into his music. This period saw him experimenting with new styles, breaking away from traditional jazz structures, and embracing a more free-form, expressive approach. *A Love Supreme*, the product of this transformation, is not just an album; it's a musical manifesto of his spiritual journey and artistic independence.

Coltrane's dedication to his craft was almost ascetic in nature. His practice sessions, often stretching for hours, were a testament to his commitment to mastery. This relentless pursuit of improvement, coupled with his openness to experimentation, led him to collaborate with a diverse array of musicians, exploring a multitude of sounds and textures. His approach to music was akin to a researcher

Productivity Smarts

constantly seeking new knowledge, pushing the boundaries of the known.

Coltrane's music was deeply intertwined with his spiritual beliefs. He saw music as more than entertainment; it was a medium for connecting souls and transcending cultural and social barriers. This profound connection to his music added an emotional depth and authenticity that resonated with his audience, making his work timeless.

John Coltrane's influence extends far beyond the realm of jazz. His explorations in music have inspired generations of musicians across genres. His willingness to incorporate diverse influences, from Indian ragas to African rhythms, broke new ground in music and laid the foundations for future musical fusions. Artists like Carlos Santana and John McLaughlin drew inspiration from his willingness to transcend traditional musical boundaries.

For the ambitious professional, Coltrane's life is a beacon, illuminating the path to success through adversity. His story teaches the power of perseverance, the importance of continuous learning, and the need for adaptability. His embrace of collaboration highlights the value of diverse perspectives and collective creativity in achieving groundbreaking results.

John Coltrane's narrative transcends music; it is a universal story of human struggle, redemption, and the relentless pursuit of excellence. His journey is a reminder that professional success is not just measured in achievements but also in the ability to continually grow, adapt, and find deeper meaning in one's work. His legacy is a testament to the idea that with dedication, open-mindedness, and a willingness to explore new avenues, one can reach unparalleled heights of success and make a lasting impact.

In an interview I did with Paul Lawrence Vann, we discussed how leaders can maximize performance in their organizations. Paul's journey into leadership and constant improvement is a masterclass in how nurturing curiosity, embracing new experiences, and seizing every learning opportunity can catapult you from a fresh recruit to a guiding light in any field. As we unpacked his story, it wasn't just about the flights or the ranks but about the mindset that propelled him through ranks and roles.

Starting with a simple summer camp that sparked his interest in the Air Force, Paul highlighted a crucial lesson for project managers: exposure to new experiences can redefine your trajectory. His narrative wasn't just about climbing the ranks but about embracing each new challenge as a stepping stone, a mindset invaluable in project management where adaptability is key.

Paul's tale of witnessing leadership evolution firsthand, from seeing a lieutenant colonel rise to a three-star general, underscores the importance of mentorship and vision in leadership. It's a vivid reminder for project managers of the power of leading by example and fostering a culture where growth and development are paramount.

But it was Paul's approach to constant improvement and experimentation that struck a chord. His career, marked by a blend of formal education and real-world experiences, illustrates the multifaceted approach to personal and professional development that is critical in project management. From formal training at the Squadron Officer School to hands-on problem-solving in high-stakes negotiations, Paul's journey is a testament to the power of combining theoretical knowledge with practical application.

His story is punctuated with moments of leadership that transcended the conventional, showing the importance of empathy, communication, and problem-solving. These are not just military virtues but are the bedrock of effective project management. Paul's narrative, especially his involvement in legislative processes and strategic negotiations, mirrors the project manager's role in navigating complex stakeholder landscapes, balancing competing interests, and steering projects to success against all odds.

What resonates most is Paul's unwavering commitment to self-improvement and his strategic approach to career development. For project managers, this is a beacon, highlighting the importance of continuous learning, adaptability, and the pursuit of excellence. Paul's ability to leverage his skills, from negotiation to strategic planning, in various contexts underscores the project manager's need for a versatile skill set that can adapt to the dynamic demands of the role.

Paul's journey from the airfields to the halls of the Pentagon embodies the ethos of project management: a relentless pursuit of growth, a strategic mindset that sees beyond the immediate, and a leadership style that inspires and empowers. His story is a compelling narrative on the importance of constant improvement and experimentation, serving as a blueprint for project managers aiming to navigate the complexities of their projects with skill, vision, and a commitment to excellence.

Paul's story, from his initial foray into the Air Force to his evolution into a respected leader, encapsulates the essence of continuous improvement and the spirit of experimentation—two pillars crucial in the realm of project management. His journey underscores a proactive approach to career development, embracing every learning opportunity and the significance of adaptability, traits that are indispensable for any project manager aiming for success in today's dynamic business environment.

The inception of Paul's career, sparked by an unexpected summer camp invitation, highlights the importance of being open to new experiences. This mirrors the project manager's need to embrace novel methodologies, technologies, and strategies to enhance project outcomes. Just as Paul's initial flight experience solidified his commitment to the Air Force, project managers often find that experimenting with new project management software, methodologies like Agile or Lean, or even team collaboration techniques can lead to breakthrough improvements in project efficiency and effectiveness.

Paul's witnessing of a colleague's rise from a lieutenant colonel to a three-star general is a testament to the impact of leadership and vision in achieving long-term success. For project managers, this translates into the importance of nurturing leadership within their teams, fostering a culture where every team member feels empowered to take initiative and contribute ideas. This culture of leadership cultivates an environment ripe for innovation, where continuous improvement becomes the norm rather than the exception.

Moreover, Paul's dedication to continuous education and skill enhancement through formal training and real-world experiences serves as a blueprint for project managers. The project management landscape is constantly evolving, with new challenges and opportunities emerging at a rapid pace. Paul's commitment to learning and adapting his skills is a powerful reminder of the need for project managers to pursue ongoing professional development, whether through certifications, workshops, or learning from each project's unique challenges.

The element of Paul's story that resonates most deeply with the ethos of project management is his strategic approach to career development, characterized by a blend of planning, flexibility, and seizing opportunities as they arise. Similarly, effective project management requires a strategic vision, the flexibility to adapt plans as projects evolve, and the agility to pivot in response to unforeseen challenges. Paul's ability to navigate the complexities of his roles, from high-stakes negotiations to legislative processes, mirrors the project manager's role in balancing competing interests, managing stakeholder expectations, and guiding projects to successful completion.

His journey is a compelling narrative on the importance of constant improvement and experimentation in project management. It illustrates how embracing change, pursuing lifelong learning, and fostering a culture of leadership and innovation can drive project success. For project managers, Paul's story serves as an inspiration to continuously seek out new knowledge, challenge the status quo, and cultivate an environment where innovation thrives, ensuring that they and their projects are always moving forward.

Productivity Smarts

For the ambitious professional, Coltrane's life is a beacon, illuminating the path to success through adversity.

In the ever-evolving landscape of modern business and project management, there exists a universal truth: the only constant is change. As a seasoned business expert with years of experience navigating the corporate world, I've witnessed firsthand the transformative power of constant improvement and experimentation. These are not just buzzwords; they are the lifeblood of successful, forward-thinking organizations.

The Need for Agility in a Dynamic Market

In today's fast-paced world, market trends, consumer preferences, and technological advancements are in a state of perpetual flux. Businesses that stand still, clinging to outdated practices and ideas, risk obsolescence. Agile businesses, on the other hand, embrace change. They view each shift in the market not as a threat but as an opportunity for growth and innovation. This agility is fueled by a dedication to constant improvement, where processes are regularly evaluated and refined.

Innovation: The Competitive Edge

Innovation is the cornerstone of competitive advantage. In a landscape crowded with competitors, the ability to innovate—to offer something unique and valuable—sets businesses apart. Experimentation is at the heart of innovation. It involves exploring new ideas, testing novel approaches, and learning from both successes and failures. By fostering a culture of experimentation, businesses can uncover breakthroughs that drive growth and profitability.

Cultivating a Resilient Workforce

A commitment to continuous improvement and experimentation also plays a crucial role in workforce development. In such environments, employees are encouraged to expand their skill sets, think creatively, and approach problems with a solutions-oriented mindset.

This not only enhances individual performance but also contributes to a more resilient and adaptable organization.

Risk Management Through Controlled Experimentation

Experimentation in business does not mean reckless risk-taking. On the contrary, it's about controlled and informed experimentation. By adopting a strategic approach to trial and error, businesses can minimize potential downsides while uncovering valuable insights. This approach is especially pertinent in project management, where the stakes are high and the success of a project can hinge on the ability to adapt and innovate.

Driving Efficiency and Reducing Waste

Continuous improvement is also key in streamlining processes and eliminating inefficiencies. In my experience, businesses that regularly review and refine their operations are more efficient, cost-effective, and productive. This relentless pursuit of efficiency often leads to significant cost savings and enhanced operational performance.

Enhancing Customer Satisfaction

In the age of the customer, meeting and exceeding customer expectations is paramount. Businesses dedicated to constant improvement are better equipped to respond to customer feedback and evolving needs. This responsiveness not only boosts customer satisfaction but also builds long-term loyalty.

Preparing for the Future

Perhaps most importantly, a dedication to constant improvement and experimentation prepares businesses for the future. It creates a foundation of flexibility and adaptability, essential qualities in an uncertain and rapidly changing world. Businesses that are constantly learning and evolving are better positioned to anticipate and respond to future challenges and opportunities.

The dedication to constant improvement and experimentation is not just a strategy for short-term gains; it is a philosophy for long-term sustainability and success. As businesses navigate the complexities of the modern market, this dedication will be a critical determinant of their ability to thrive in an unpredictable future. Those who embrace this ethos will lead the way, charting a course through uncharted waters with confidence and resilience.

Research in psychology, neuroscience, and business consistently underscores the importance of being dedicated to constant improvement and experimentation. Here's a deeper dive into why this commitment is so valuable:

1. Psychology: The Growth Mindset and Resilience

Growth Mindset Theory (Carol Dweck, Stanford University)

Carol Dweck's research on the "growth mindset" shows that individuals who believe their abilities can be developed through dedication and hard work are more likely to embrace challenges, learn from criticism, and persist in the face of setbacks. This mindset fosters a love for learning and resilience, which are essential for personal and professional growth.

Key Findings: Dweck's studies have demonstrated that people with a growth mindset outperform those with a fixed mindset, even when they start at a similar level. This is because they view challenges as opportunities to learn rather than threats to their competence.

Self-Determination Theory (Edward Deci and Richard Ryan, University of Rochester)

Self-Determination Theory (SDT) emphasizes the role of intrinsic motivation—motivation that comes from within rather than from external rewards. Deci and Ryan's research shows that when individuals feel a sense of autonomy, competence, and relatedness, they are more motivated to pursue self-improvement and engage in experimentation. This leads to higher productivity, creativity, and job satisfaction.

Key Findings: Organizations that support autonomy and encourage a culture of learning and growth see higher levels of employee engagement, creativity, and innovation.

2. Neuroscience: Brain Plasticity and Innovation

Neuroplasticity: The Brain's Ability to Change and Adapt
Neuroscience research highlights that the brain is highly plastic, meaning it has the ability to reorganize itself by forming new neural connections throughout life. Constant learning and experimentation stimulate this neuroplasticity, leading to cognitive flexibility, improved problem-solving abilities, and enhanced creativity.

Key Findings: Studies have shown that activities that challenge the brain—such as learning a new language, playing a musical instrument, or engaging in novel problem-solving tasks—can increase the density of gray matter in the brain and improve cognitive functions such as memory, attention, and decision-making (Draganski et al., 2004).

The Role of Dopamine in Learning and Motivation
Dopamine, a neurotransmitter, plays a critical role in motivation,

learning, and the reward system. Research by Schultz et al. (1997) has demonstrated that dopamine is released when we encounter new and rewarding experiences. This release encourages further exploration, experimentation, and the pursuit of new challenges.

Key Findings: The brain's reward circuitry encourages behaviors that lead to learning and growth, reinforcing the benefits of constant improvement and experimentation. This is why individuals who regularly seek new challenges and push themselves beyond their comfort zones often feel more fulfilled and motivated in their professional lives.

3. Business: Innovation, Performance, and Competitive Advantage

Organizational Learning Theory (Chris Argyris and Donald Schön)

Argyris and Schön's theory emphasizes that organizations that continually learn and adapt are better positioned to innovate and respond to changes in the market. This theory highlights the importance of "double-loop learning," where organizations not only solve problems but also question and modify their underlying assumptions and values.

Key Findings: Businesses that encourage continuous learning and experimentation among employees tend to have higher innovation rates, better adaptability, and more sustained competitive advantages. A culture that embraces failure as a learning opportunity is crucial for fostering innovation.

The Boston Consulting Group (BCG) Innovation Report (2020)

BCG's annual report on the most innovative companies found that organizations that prioritize experimentation, rapid prototyping, and iterative learning are more likely to achieve higher growth rates and profitability. According to the report, 60% of the most innovative companies in 2020 encouraged their employees to spend time on side projects and exploration.

Key Findings: Companies with a strong culture of innovation—where constant improvement and experimentation are core values—experienced almost twice the revenue growth of their less innovative counterparts. They also had significantly higher employee engagement and retention rates.

Research from the *Harvard Business Review* (*HBR*) on Psychological Safety (Amy Edmondson, Harvard Business School)

Amy Edmondson's research on psychological safety in teams found that teams on which members feel safe to take risks, share ideas, and learn from failures are more innovative and productive. Psychological safety is crucial for fostering an environment where experimentation and continuous improvement are not only accepted but encouraged.

Key Findings: Teams with high psychological safety are more likely to engage in "knowledge-sharing" behaviors, leading to improved decision-making, creativity, and performance. This supports a culture of continuous learning and experimentation.

Conclusion: The Integrated View

Research from psychology, neuroscience, and business consistently shows that being dedicated to constant improvement and experimentation is essential for personal and organizational success. It fosters a growth mindset, enhances brain function and adaptability, drives innovation, and creates a competitive edge in the market.

How can you foster a growth mindset in yourself and your team?

What areas in your professional life could benefit from more experimentation and continuous learning?

How can you make time in your busy schedule for innovation and creative problem-solving?

Are there any current setbacks or challenges you could view as opportunities for growth?

Drawing inspiration from John Coltrane's life and approach to music, we can derive practical steps for incorporating his dedication to constant improvement and experimentation into project management. These steps can help foster a culture of innovation, resilience, and growth in any project team.

Step 1: Cultivate a Growth Mindset

- **Encourage Continuous Learning:** Just as Coltrane never stopped learning and evolving, promote ongoing education and skill development within your team.

- **Provide Resources:** Offer access to training, workshops, and seminars relevant to your project and industry.

Step 2: Embrace Challenges as Opportunities

- **Foster Resilience:** When facing project setbacks, encourage the team to see them as opportunities for growth and learning, much like Coltrane's approach to his personal challenges.
- **Problem-Solving Sessions:** Regularly hold brainstorming sessions to tackle project issues creatively and constructively.

Step 3: Encourage Creative Problem-Solving

- **Innovation Workshops:** Regularly schedule sessions where team members can freely brainstorm and experiment with new ideas without the pressure of immediate practical application.
- **Reward Creativity:** Acknowledge and reward creative solutions and innovative approaches within the team.

Step 4: Promote Deep Engagement with Work

- **Connect Work to Larger Goals:** Help team members understand how their individual roles contribute to the broader objectives of the project, much like how Coltrane viewed his music as part of a larger spiritual journey.
- **Encourage Passion Projects:** Allow team members to spend a portion of their time on projects they are passionate about that also benefit the team or company.

Step 5: Foster an Environment of Open Collaboration

- **Collaborative Spaces:** Create physical or virtual spaces where team members can easily collaborate and share ideas.
- **Cross-functional Teams:** Encourage team members to work in cross-functional teams, bringing diverse perspectives and skills to the table.

Step 6: Practice Reflective Learning

- **Regular Reviews:** Implement a process for regular project reviews, where the team reflects on successes, challenges, and lessons learned.
- **Personal Reflection:** Encourage individual team members to reflect on their own performance and growth.

Step 7: Encourage Diversity of Thought and Experience

- **Diverse Team Composition:** Build a team with diverse backgrounds and skill sets, reflecting Coltrane's eclectic musical influences.
- **Cultural Exchange Sessions:** Organize sessions where team members can share their diverse experiences and perspectives.

Step 8: Set Clear, Evolving Goals

- **Dynamic Goal-Setting:** Set project goals but be open to evolving them as the project progresses, mirroring Coltrane's fluid approach to his musical career.

- **Individual Goals:** Help team members set and regularly review their own professional goals.

Step 9: Create a Culture of Openness and Feedback

- **Regular Feedback Mechanisms:** Establish a culture where constructive feedback is regularly exchanged among team members.
- **Open Door Policy:** Encourage open communication lines between team members and management.

Step 10: Balance Discipline with Flexibility

- **Structured Flexibility:** While maintaining a structured approach to project management, remain flexible to new ideas and changes in the project's direction.
- **Personal Autonomy:** Give team members autonomy in their work while ensuring they adhere to project guidelines and deadlines.

By integrating these steps into project management, inspired by John Coltrane's dedication to improvement and experimentation, project teams can foster an environment that encourages growth, resilience, and innovative problem-solving.

Exercise 1: Growth Mindset Workshop
Objective: Cultivate a culture of continuous learning and adaptability.

- **Step 1:** Begin with a presentation on the concept of a growth mindset, using examples from Coltrane's career.

- **Step 2:** Conduct group discussions where team members share personal experiences of overcoming challenges.
- **Step 3:** Facilitate a workshop to identify areas for personal and professional growth within the team.
- **Step 4:** Develop individual action plans for team members to pursue their identified growth areas.

Exercise 2: Creative Problem-Solving Hackathon
Objective: Foster innovative thinking and creative solutions to project challenges.

- **Step 1:** Present a specific project challenge to the team.
- **Step 2:** Divide the team into small groups to brainstorm creative solutions.
- **Step 3:** Reconvene for each group to present their ideas.
- **Step 4:** Vote on the most innovative solutions and discuss how to implement them in the project.

Exercise 3: Reflective Learning Session
Objective: Encourage reflection on past experiences for continuous improvement.

- **Step 1:** Ask team members to reflect on a recent project or task and write down key learnings.
- **Step 2:** Facilitate a group discussion where each member shares their insights.
- **Step 3:** Identify common themes and lessons that can be applied to future projects.
- **Step 4:** Create a "lessons learned" document for the team to reference.

Exercise 4: Cross-Functional Collaboration Exercise
Objective: Enhance teamwork and collaboration across different functions.

- **Step 1:** Create mixed teams with members from different functional areas.
- **Step 2:** Assign a mini-project or problem that requires input from various specialties.
- **Step 3:** Monitor the teams as they work together, offering guidance as needed.
- **Step 4:** Hold a debrief session to discuss what worked well and what challenges were encountered.

Exercise 5: Goal-Setting and Review Workshop
Objective: Set clear, evolving goals aligned with individual and team growth.

- **Step 1:** Introduce the concept of SMART goals.
- **Step 2:** Guide team members in setting personal and professional goals.
- **Step 3:** Develop a process for regular review and adjustment of these goals.
- **Step 4:** Schedule periodic check-ins to monitor progress and provide support.

Exercise 6: Openness and Feedback Culture Building
Objective: Create a supportive environment for open communication and constructive feedback.

- **Step 1:** Host a session on effective communication and feedback techniques.
- **Step 2:** Engage in role-playing exercises to practice giving and receiving feedback.

- **Step 3:** Implement a regular feedback mechanism in your team's routine.
- **Step 4:** Encourage ongoing, informal feedback exchanges among team members.

Exercise 7: Diversity of Thought Session

Objective: Appreciate and leverage the diverse perspectives within the team.

- **Step 1:** Have each team member share something unique about their background or approach to work.
- **Step 2:** Discuss how these diverse viewpoints can enhance problem-solving and creativity.
- **Step 3:** Identify opportunities for incorporating diverse perspectives in ongoing projects.
- **Step 4:** Establish a practice of regularly seeking and valuing diverse opinions in team discussions.

By regularly conducting these exercises, you can instill a culture of continuous improvement, creative problem-solving, and effective collaboration, much like the ethos that drove John Coltrane to greatness in his field.

Transform your workplace culture into a symphony of collaboration and innovation—subscribe today:

Part Four
Pillar Four – Collaboration and Vulnerability

The Power of Connection

In a world where innovation and productivity often take center stage, collaboration and vulnerability serve as the glue that binds individuals and teams together. Collaboration is more than working alongside others; it's about creating an environment where diverse talents, perspectives, and ideas converge to achieve something greater than any individual could accomplish alone. Vulnerability, often misunderstood as a weakness, is its powerful counterpart. It is the willingness to be open, to share struggles and emotions, and to build trust—laying the foundation for meaningful connections and authentic teamwork.

Collaboration and vulnerability are the heart of high-functioning teams. They allow us to move beyond transactional interactions to create relationships rooted in mutual respect, understanding, and shared purpose. When these principles are embraced, they transform workplaces into dynamic spaces where creativity thrives, innovation flourishes, and people feel genuinely valued.

Rihanna, Justin Timberlake, and Billie Eilish exemplify the transformative power of collaboration and vulnerability. Through their unique approaches, they have redefined what it means to work with others, highlighting the importance of openness, effort, and emotional intelligence in achieving greatness.

Rihanna's career is a testament to the art of collaboration. From her ventures in music, fashion, and beauty to her partnerships with some of the biggest names in the industry, Rihanna has mastered the ability to bring people and ideas together. Her ability to collaborate effectively across disciplines stems from her openness to diverse perspectives and her focus on shared goals. Rihanna's success shows that collaboration isn't just about working well with others—it's about fostering an environment where everyone feels empowered to contribute their best. In the workplace, this translates to building harmonious teams that function as cohesive units, leveraging the unique strengths of each member to achieve outstanding results.

Justin Timberlake offers a lesson in balancing individual effort with collaborative success. While Timberlake is a celebrated solo artist, his career has been marked by collaborations that elevate his work and the work of those around him. From his early days in *NSYNC to partnerships with artists across genres, Timberlake's ability to collaborate tirelessly while maintaining his high standards of excellence demonstrates how personal dedication can coexist with collective achievement. His example teaches us that collaboration is not about compromising individuality—it's about combining individual strengths to create something greater than the sum of its parts.

Billie Eilish brings another dimension to this pillar: the strength of vulnerability. Eilish's willingness to share her emotions and struggles through her music has forged deep connections with her audience. Her openness demonstrates that vulnerability is not a liability but a powerful tool for building trust and fostering genuine relationships. In the workplace, vulnerability allows leaders and team members to communicate authentically, acknowledge challenges, and create an environment where people feel safe to take risks, share ideas, and support one another. Emotional intelligence, rooted in empathy and self-awareness, becomes the cornerstone of effective teamwork.

The lessons from these icons highlight the transformative potential of collaboration and vulnerability. Rihanna teaches us to embrace diverse perspectives and foster harmony in teams. Timberlake reminds us to balance individual effort with collective achievement, ensuring that both personal and team goals are met. Eilish shows us the power of openness, demonstrating that authenticity and emotional intelligence are vital for building trust and connection.

As you reflect on this pillar, consider how these principles apply to your own professional context. Are you fostering a collaborative culture where diverse voices are valued and encouraged? Are you balancing individual contributions with team goals? Are you leading with vulnerability, creating an environment where trust and authenticity thrive? These questions can guide you in building teams and relationships that are not only effective but also deeply fulfilling.

In the chapters ahead, we'll explore how to integrate these lessons into your work. From fostering collaboration inspired by Rihanna and Timberlake to embracing vulnerability as modeled by Eilish, you'll gain actionable insights into creating stronger, more connected teams. Whether you're managing a project, leading a team, or navigating interpersonal relationships, this pillar will provide the tools to build trust, cultivate empathy, and achieve success through connection.

Collaboration and vulnerability are not just the foundation of teamwork—they are the keys to creating a workplace culture that values people as much as outcomes. With inspiration from Rihanna, Timberlake, and Eilish, you'll discover how to lead with openness, connect with authenticity, and achieve greatness through the power of connection. The journey to building meaningful relationships and high-functioning teams begins here.

Chapter 10
Rihanna

O ne of Rihanna's productivity superpowers is her ability to collaborate effectively with others.

"I think a lot of people are afraid of being great because of the power and responsibility that come with it. I love to work with people who aren't afraid to grow, aren't afraid to be great, and I thrive off that energy." —Rihanna

Rihanna is an artist who has not only left an indelible mark on the music industry but has also become a symbol of collaborative brilliance. Rihanna's story is one of unparalleled success, innovation, and a unique talent for bringing together diverse creative forces.

Born Robyn Rihanna Fenty in Saint Michael, Barbados, in 1988, Rihanna's early life hinted at the resilience and determination that would later define her career. Discovered by a talent scout at the age of 15, she ventured into the music industry with a distinctive blend of Caribbean influences and R&B.

From the beginning, Rihanna showcased an openness to collaboration that set her apart. Her debut single, "Pon de Replay," not only became a chart-topping hit but also marked the beginning of a career characterized by a willingness to explore new sounds and styles. Rihanna's ability to seamlessly incorporate elements from various genres laid the foundation for her collaborative prowess.

One of the defining moments in Rihanna's collaborative journey was her partnership with Jay-Z's Roc Nation. Under his mentorship, she flourished not just as a performer but as a curator of musical experiences. Her early collaborations with established artists like Jay-Z and Sean Paul hinted at a star on the rise, but it was the release of her third studio album, *Good Girl Gone Bad*, that catapulted her to global superstardom.

The album's lead single, "Umbrella," featuring Jay-Z, not only became an anthem but showcased Rihanna's knack for choosing collaborators strategically. The chemistry between her and Jay-Z was palpable, setting the stage for future collaborations that would redefine the pop and R&B landscapes.

Rihanna's ability to collaborate effectively expanded beyond the music studio. Her venture into fashion with PUMA and later Fenty Beauty demonstrated a commitment to inclusivity and diversity. With Fenty Beauty, Rihanna not only revolutionized the beauty industry but set a new standard for collaborative ventures between celebrities and major brands.

The album *Rated R* marked another turning point in Rihanna's career. Collaborating with producers and artists such as Ne-Yo, will.i.am, and Justin Timberlake, she delivered an album that delved into darker themes while maintaining mainstream appeal. The willingness to explore new sonic territories and collaborate with a diverse array of talent showcased Rihanna's artistic maturity.

Her collaborative endeavors continued to evolve with the release of *Loud* and *Talk That Talk*, featuring collaborations with Calvin Harris, Drake, and Eminem. The latter's "Love the Way You Lie" became a global phenomenon, underscoring Rihanna's ability to lend her voice to emotionally charged collaborations.

Rihanna's later albums, including *Anti* and *Unapologetic*, further solidified her reputation for innovative collaborations. Working with artists like SZA, Travis Scott, and Drake, she effortlessly navigated the intersections of pop, R&B, and hip-hop, consistently surprising audiences with her adaptability.

Beyond music and fashion, Rihanna's collaboration with the Clara Lionel Foundation highlighted her commitment to philanthropy. By bringing together various organizations and individuals, she demonstrated how collaboration can be a force for positive change.

Rihanna's collaborative spirit serves as a beacon of inspiration. Whether it's in the studio, the boardroom, or through philanthropic initiatives, Rihanna's ability to unite diverse talents has not only shaped her career but has also set a standard for collaborative excellence.

I recall a pivotal moment at the age of 12 when I joined my first band. This experience, which I shared in my TEDx talk, was a significant turning point, not just in my musical journey but in shaping my understanding of collaboration and leadership. Behind me, as I spoke, was a little red guitar, a symbol of my initial foray into music. I had started learning the piano, but the allure of the guitar was irresistible. However, my aspirations of playing guitar in the band were quickly overshadowed by a bandmate whose skills rivaled those of Jimi Hendrix. This realization led me to the bass guitar, a decision that would profoundly influence my approach to teamwork and leadership.

Learning to play the bass was not just about mastering an instrument; it was about understanding the essence of collaboration. The bass required me to learn the entirety of a song, to continuously play, supporting everyone else in the band. This role taught me the importance of laying down the foundation, of being the groove that everything else builds upon. To improve, I sought out a skilled bass teacher, a decision that underscored the value of continuous learning and dedication. This journey was not just about music; it was a metaphor for growth, both personal and professional.

The parallels between music and business are striking. Playing in a band taught me the critical skill of listening—not just hearing, but truly understanding what others are contributing. In the business environment, listening often becomes a secondary concern, with individuals more focused on their response than on understanding and blending with the ideas of others. However, true collaboration, much like making music, requires us to listen with the intent to understand and complement.

As a bass player, my role was to support and provide the foundation that allowed others to shine. This notion of support translated seamlessly into my role as a CEO, where the essence of leadership is not about being in the spotlight but about enabling others to excel. Leadership, I learned, is about surrendering to the role of supporter, ensuring that each team member has what they need to succeed. These lessons from music became the cornerstone of my approach to business, emphasizing the importance of teamwork, active listening, and the continuous pursuit of improvement.

My appearance on C-Suite TV and discussions about my book *Symphony of Choices* further explore these concepts. The analogy of a symphony to business resonates deeply with me, despite not being a musician by professional training. In a symphony, as in business, each participant must listen carefully, understanding when to step forward and when to blend into the background, all under the guidance of a leader-conductor. This harmony, the balance of individual contributions and collective performance, is essential for creating impactful, lasting success.

Through my journey from a young musician to a TEDx speaker and author, the lessons learned from music have profoundly shaped my perspective on business and leadership. The principles of effective collaboration, the art of listening, and the importance of supporting others are not just musical concepts but are fundamental to leading and succeeding in any endeavor. My experience underscores the belief that the most harmonious outcomes, whether in music or in business, arise from a symphony of choices, where every note, every decision, contributes to the creation of something truly extraordinary.

"I love working with talented people. When you surround yourself with good people, you naturally grow." —Selena Gomez (musician)

The importance of collaborating effectively in portfolio and project management is underscored by the remarkable careers of individuals like Rihanna, who has become a paragon of collaborative success in the music industry, and my own experiences, which I've shared from stages and in my writings, including my TEDx talk and the book *Symphony of Choices*. Rihanna's journey from a young talent in Barbados to a global superstar highlights the power of bringing together diverse talents and visions to create something unparalleled. My own journey, starting with a simple red guitar and evolving through the complex dynamics of playing in a band, parallels this ethos in the realm of business and leadership.

Rihanna's career is a testament to the significance of collaboration, showing how it can lead to innovation, growth, and groundbreaking achievements. Her ability to blend different genres and work with a wide range of artists and producers has not only defined her as a musical icon but also as a visionary in the fashion and beauty industries. Her work with Jay-Z, for example, wasn't just about creating hit songs; it was about mutual learning and pushing boundaries. Similarly, her ventures into fashion with PUMA and beauty with Fenty Beauty have set new standards for inclusivity and diversity, showcasing how collaborative efforts can lead to industry-wide changes.

Drawing from my experiences, joining a band taught me the foundational skills of listening, supporting, and blending different talents toward a common goal. The transition from wanting to be a guitarist to finding my niche as a bass player highlighted the essence of finding one's role within a team and excelling in it to support collective success. This musical journey, much like Rihanna's, emphasizes the need for continuous learning, adaptation, and the willingness to explore new territories.

In both music and business, the art of listening is paramount. True collaboration requires us to listen with the intent to understand and integrate rather than just respond. This skill is critical in project management, where the success of initiatives often hinges on the team's ability to synthesize diverse perspectives and expertise toward a unified goal. My role as a bass player, focusing on supporting others, directly translates to leadership and management practices where the goal is to empower and uplift the team to achieve collective success.

Moreover, Rihanna's engagement in philanthropy and my discussions on leadership and choice underscore the broader implications of collaboration. It's about creating a positive impact that extends beyond individual success to benefit wider communities and industries. Effective collaboration in portfolio and project management is not just about completing projects efficiently; it's about fostering an environment where innovation, creativity, and mutual respect thrive.

Whether it's in the studio, in the boardroom, or on the global stage, the ability to work effectively with others, to listen deeply, and to support each other's strengths is what drives transformative outcomes. In the end, the most harmonious outcomes in music, business, or any field are achieved through a symphony of choices, where every contribution is valued, and every collaboration is a step toward something truly extraordinary.

"If everyone is moving forward together, then success takes care of itself." —Henry Ford

"Teamwork makes the dream work, but a vision becomes a nightmare when the leader has a big dream and a bad team." —John C. Maxwell

"None of us is as smart as all of us." —Ken Blanchard

How do I contribute to creating a positive and productive team environment?

Am I open to listening to others' ideas, and how do I show that I value their input?

How do I handle conflicts or disagreements within a team, and do I strive for resolution?

What can I do to build stronger trust and rapport with my colleagues or team members?

How do I adapt my communication style to work effectively with different personalities?

What steps can I take to ensure that everyone feels included and valued in a group project?

Do I actively support and encourage my teammates, especially during challenging moments?

How do I balance my own ideas and ambitions with the needs and goals of the team?

Am I reliable and consistent in fulfilling my responsibilities within a group setting?

What can I learn from others on my team that can help me grow both personally and professionally?

Let's translate Rihanna's ability to collaborate effectively into practical steps for project management:

1. **Identify Project Goals:**
    - **Action:** Clearly articulate project goals and objectives.

- **Rationale:** Setting clear goals provides a shared vision, aligning the team toward a common purpose.
2. **Diverse Team Composition:**
    - **Action:** Assemble a team with diverse skills and backgrounds.
    - **Rationale:** Diverse teams bring varied perspectives, fostering creativity and comprehensive problem-solving.
3. **Effective Communication Channels:**
    - **Action:** Establish communication channels using tools like Slack or Microsoft Teams.
    - **Rationale:** Transparent communication ensures everyone is on the same page, reducing misunderstandings.
4. **Project Management Tools:**
    - **Action:** Implement project management tools such as Asana for task organization.
    - **Rationale:** Tools streamline workflows, enhancing organization and efficiency in project management.
5. **Task Delegation Based on Strengths:**
    - **Action:** Assign tasks aligning with team members' strengths.
    - **Rationale:** Leveraging individual strengths maximizes efficiency and quality in task execution.
6. **Creative Collaboration Environment:**
    - **Action:** Foster a creative atmosphere where team members feel comfortable sharing ideas.
    - **Rationale:** Creativity flourishes in an environment that encourages open expression and experimentation.
7. **Parallel Workstreams:**
    - **Action:** Divide tasks into parallel workstreams for simultaneous progress.

- **Rationale:** Parallel work accelerates project timelines and prevents bottlenecks.
8. **Feedback and Iteration:**
    - **Action:** Establish regular feedback sessions for continuous improvement.
    - **Rationale:** Feedback loops enhance quality by incorporating insights and learning throughout the project.
9. **Adaptability to Changes:**
    - **Action:** Embrace adaptability to changes in project requirements.
    - **Rationale:** Flexibility allows the team to respond effectively to evolving project needs.
10. **Regular Team Check-Ins:**
    - **Action:** Schedule routine team check-ins to discuss progress and challenges.
    - **Rationale:** Regular check-ins maintain alignment, address issues promptly, and foster a collaborative culture.
11. **Collaborative Platforms for Creativity:**
    - **Action:** Utilize collaborative platforms like Google Workspace for real-time interaction.
    - **Rationale:** These tools facilitate synchronous collaboration, enhancing creativity and efficiency.
12. **Effective Time Management:**
    - **Action:** Set realistic timelines and encourage effective time allocation.
    - **Rationale:** Proper time management prevents delays and ensures project milestones are met.
13. **Celebrating Collaborative Success:**
    - **Action:** Acknowledge and celebrate collaborative milestones.
    - **Rationale:** Recognizing achievements boosts team morale and reinforces a culture of success.

14. **Learning from Collaborations:**
    - **Action:** Conduct post-project evaluations to extract learnings.
    - **Rationale:** Continuous learning optimizes future collaborations by identifying successful strategies and areas for improvement.
15. **Strategic External Collaborations:**
    - **Action:** Consider external collaborations for specialized expertise.
    - **Rationale:** External collaborations bring in fresh perspectives and skills, enhancing project outcomes.

By taking these actions, you can create a collaborative project management environment that mirrors the effective collaboration seen in Rihanna's career. This approach fosters creativity, ensures efficient workflows, and leads to successful project delivery.

Step-by-step exercises to reinforce the principles of effective collaboration in project management:

Exercise 1: Team Building Workshop
Objective: Build strong team dynamics and enhance collaboration.

1. **Action:**
   - **Organize a Team Building Workshop:**
     - Include icebreaker activities, team-building exercises, and interactive sessions.
     - Encourage open communication and collaboration throughout the workshop.
2. **Rationale:**
   - **Team Cohesion:**
     - Builds rapport among team members.
     - Enhances trust and communication.

Exercise 2: Virtual Collaboration Simulation
Objective: Develop skills for effective virtual collaboration.

1. **Action:**
   - **Simulate a Virtual Project:**
     - Assign tasks to team members using virtual collaboration tools.
     - Emphasize communication through virtual channels.
2. **Rationale:**
   - **Adaptability:**
     - Prepares the team for remote work scenarios.
     - Enhances familiarity with virtual collaboration tools.

Exercise 3: Task Delegation Challenge
Objective: Practice strategic task delegation based on team members' strengths.

1. **Action:**
   - **Identify Team Strengths:**
     - Conduct a skills assessment for each team member.
     - Delegate tasks aligning with individual strengths.
2. **Rationale:**
   - **Efficient Task Execution:**
     - Maximizes productivity by leveraging individual capabilities.
     - Encourages collaboration based on expertise.

Productivity Smarts

Exercise 4: Collaborative Decision-Making
Objective: Strengthen collaborative decision-making skills.

1. **Action:**
   - **Simulate Decision-Making Scenarios:**
     - Present hypothetical project decisions.
     - Encourage team discussion and collaborative decision-making.
2. **Rationale:**
   - **Consensus Building:**
     - Enhances the team's ability to make collective decisions.
     - Fosters a sense of shared responsibility.

Exercise 5: Continuous Improvement Feedback Session
Objective: Establish a culture of continuous improvement through feedback.

1. **Action:**
   - **Schedule Regular Feedback Sessions:**
     - Conduct feedback sessions after key project milestones.
     - Discuss successes, challenges, and areas for improvement.
2. **Rationale:**
   - **Learning Culture:**
     - Promotes a culture of continuous improvement.
     - Provides insights for refining collaborative strategies.

Exercise 6: External Collaboration Case Study
Objective: Explore the benefits of external collaborations.

1. **Action:**
   - **Assign a Case Study:**
     - Provide a case study on successful external collaborations in your industry.
     - Discuss the impact on project outcomes.
2. **Rationale:**
   - **Strategic Collaboration:**
     - Encourages teams to consider external collaborations strategically.
     - Expands awareness of collaborative possibilities.

Exercise 7: Project Closure Reflection
Objective: Reflect on the collaborative journey at the project closure.

1. **Action:**
   - **Conduct a Project Closure Reflection:**
     - Schedule a reflection session at the end of the project.
     - Discuss collaborative successes, challenges, and lessons learned.
2. **Rationale:**
   - **Knowledge Transfer:**
     - Captures insights for future projects.
     - Reinforces a culture of continuous learning and improvement.

These exercises are designed to reinforce collaborative principles,

Productivity Smarts

from team building to effective decision-making. Incorporating them into your project management practices will contribute to a collaborative and high-performing team.

Learn how to track the right metrics and stay on course toward success—start here:

Chapter 11
Justin Timberlake

He became known for his productivity superpower—his ability to work tirelessly to achieve his goals while still maintaining a collaborative and open-minded approach to his work.

"I really try to take the approach of letting the music do the talking and try to be open to working with talented people because collaboration can bring out the best ideas." —Justin Timberlake

Productivity Smarts

. . .

In the vibrant city of Memphis, Tennessee, a young prodigy named Justin Timberlake was destined to make an indelible mark on the world of entertainment. Born in 1981, Justin's journey from local talent to a global icon is a testament to his extraordinary work ethic, unparalleled creativity, and remarkable ability to seamlessly balance individual pursuit with collaborative excellence.

Hailing from a working-class family, Justin's early exposure to the world of entertainment came through his participation in the Mickey Mouse Club. Even at a young age, he exhibited a natural talent for performance and a passion for music that would shape his future endeavors.

The pivotal moment in Justin's career arrived with the formation of *NSYNC, a boy band that would become a phenomenon in the late 1990s and early 2000s. As the group rose to unprecedented fame, Justin's dedication to his craft became increasingly evident. Beyond his role as a vocalist, he actively engaged in songwriting and production, showcasing a multifaceted skill set that hinted at his future solo success.

However, Justin's transition to a solo career marked a significant turning point. Recognizing the need for creative exploration and personal growth, he made the bold decision to step into the spotlight on his own terms. This transition not only solidified his status as a solo artist but marked the beginning of an era defined by his distinct musical style, blending R&B influences with innovative production.

What set Justin apart was not just his individual brilliance but his commitment to collaboration. His debut solo album, *Justified*, was a testament to his openness to working with diverse talents. Collaborations with renowned hip-hop producer Timbaland resulted in a groundbreaking fusion of pop, R&B, and electronic elements, setting the stage for future successes.

The release of *FutureSex/LoveSounds* further established Justin as a solo powerhouse. His tireless work ethic was evident in the meticulous crafting of each track, pushing the boundaries of mainstream pop music. The album's success was a testament to Justin's ability to evolve creatively while staying true to his roots, showcasing an artistic maturity that resonated with audiences worldwide.

Beyond the confines of the recording studio, Justin's ventures into acting and entrepreneurship reflected his multifaceted approach to success. His roles in films like *The Social Network* demonstrated his versatility as an artist, while his entrepreneurial ventures, including the fashion label William Rast, showcased his business acumen.

Justin's impact extends far beyond accolades and record sales. His collaborative spirit manifested in iconic duets, such as "SexyBack" with Timbaland and "Suit & Tie" with Jay-Z. These partnerships not only demonstrated his ability to blend genres seamlessly but also showcased his capacity to create music that resonated with a diverse global audience.

As a solo artist, actor, and entrepreneur, Justin Timberlake embodies the essence of hard work, adaptability, and collaboration. His commitment to perfection and his ability to embrace innovation while maintaining an open-minded approach has solidified his place in the annals of entertainment history.

Justin's story serves as an inspiration for those navigating the complexities of a dynamic career. His relentless pursuit of excellence, combined with a collaborative spirit, showcases the power of staying true to oneself while remaining open to the transformative potential of collaboration. In the symphony of his career, Justin Timberlake continues to hit the right notes, leaving an indelible mark on the world of entertainment.

In the fast-paced world of project and portfolio management, I've come to understand the importance of perseverance and resilience when it comes to achieving long-term goals. Success in any project requires the ability to work tirelessly, staying focused on the end result while not allowing short-term setbacks to throw you off course.

Productivity Smarts

This kind of dedication is crucial, not just for personal success but for the success of the entire team, because each project is a stepping stone toward fulfilling a larger organizational vision.

At the same time, I believe strongly in the power of collaboration. While having a strong work ethic can certainly drive progress, it's the collective effort of a team that ensures a project's ultimate success. I've learned that the best ideas often emerge when we're open to diverse perspectives and willing to listen. No matter how much experience I bring to the table, there's always something valuable I can learn from others, and that openness to new ideas can make all the difference in how efficiently and creatively we meet our goals.

As a leader, I see collaboration as essential. It's not just about directing the team—it's about empowering each member to contribute their unique expertise. When we create an environment where everyone feels valued and heard, morale increases and so does productivity. I've seen firsthand that when people feel like they're part of something bigger and their input is appreciated, the team becomes capable of exceeding expectations.

For me, project and portfolio management is about more than just hard work—it's about fostering a culture of collaboration. By working together and staying open to new ideas, we can take on any challenge and reach even the most ambitious goals. No project is too complex when you have a team aligned and working toward a common purpose.

"The strength of the team is each individual member. The strength of each member is the team." — Phil Jackson

The superpower of being able to work tirelessly to achieve goals while still maintaining a collaborative and open-minded approach is essential in business for several key reasons.

First, the ability to work tirelessly reflects a strong commitment to success and resilience in the face of challenges. In business, goals are often ambitious, and setbacks are inevitable. Someone who can push through those obstacles with relentless focus is more likely to reach their objectives. This work ethic not only drives individual success but also sets a powerful example for others in the organization, fostering a culture of perseverance and dedication.

However, working tirelessly without collaboration can limit growth. Business today is increasingly complex, and no one person has all the answers. Maintaining a collaborative approach allows leaders and team members to tap into the collective intelligence of the group, leading to better problem-solving and innovation. When you combine tireless work with an open-minded, team-oriented mindset, you create an environment where people feel their contributions matter, which boosts motivation and engagement.

Being open-minded is also crucial because it encourages adaptability. In a constantly evolving business landscape, being open to new ideas and perspectives enables leaders to pivot when necessary and seize opportunities that others might miss. It helps teams avoid tunnel vision and find creative solutions, making businesses more agile and competitive.

Ultimately, this combination of hard work, collaboration, and openness creates a winning formula for long-term success. It's not just about pushing harder—it's about working smarter, leveraging the strengths of the team, and staying flexible enough to evolve with changing circumstances.

"None of us, including me, ever do great things. But we can all do small things, with great love, and together we can do something wonderful." —Mother Teresa

"The strength of the team is each individual member. The strength of each member is the team." —Phil Jackson

Productivity Smarts

"Great things happen when you're open to new ideas and collaboration with others because creativity is often born from different perspectives coming together." —Alicia Keys (musician)

"Teamwork is the ability to work together toward a common vision. The ability to direct individual accomplishments toward organizational objectives. It is the fuel that allows common people to attain uncommon results." —Andrew Carnegie

How do I balance working hard toward my personal goals with being open to input and collaboration from others?

Am I willing to adapt my ideas or strategies when others contribute valuable perspectives, or do I hold onto my original plans too tightly?

How can I create an environment where collaboration enhances the quality of my work rather than feeling like it compromises my vision?

When working with others, how do I ensure that I stay focused on achieving my goals without losing sight of the team's objectives?

How do I maintain a mindset of openness and curiosity when collaborating, especially if others' ideas challenge my own?

In what ways can collaboration help me achieve my goals faster or more effectively than working alone?

How do I handle situations where collaboration doesn't go as planned while still maintaining a positive, open-minded attitude?

How can I balance pushing toward my own goals with ensuring that others feel their contributions are valued and heard?

Am I surrounding myself with people who challenge me to grow and think differently, and how does that impact my work ethic and creativity?

How do I foster strong working relationships while remaining focused and determined to pursue my personal and professional goals?

Incorporating Justin Timberlake's work ethic and collaborative approach into project management can be a transformative experience. Here are practical steps inspired by his journey:

Step 1: Define Your Vision

- **Action:** Clearly articulate the vision and goals of your project.
- **Rationale:** Justin's success stems from a clear vision. Define what success looks like for your project to guide every decision.

Step 2: Embrace Multifaceted Skills

- **Action:** Encourage team members to diversify their skill sets.
- **Rationale:** Justin's ability to sing, write, and produce showcases the power of versatility. A well-rounded team can adapt to challenges more effectively.

Step 3: Foster Open Communication

- **Action:** Establish an open communication culture within the team.
- **Rationale:** Justin's collaborations thrive on communication. Encouraging openness ensures that ideas flow freely, leading to innovative solutions.

Step 4: Encourage Creative Exploration

- **Action:** Create an environment that allows for creative exploration.
- **Rationale:** Justin's solo career was marked by innovation. Permitting creative freedom fosters a culture of continuous improvement.

Step 5: Emphasize Collaboration

- **Action:** Promote collaboration across departments or teams.
- **Rationale:** Justin's collaborations transcend genres. Encouraging cross-functional collaboration enhances problem-solving and brings diverse perspectives to the table.

Step 6: Adaptability Is Key

- **Action:** Cultivate adaptability within the team.

- **Rationale:** Justin's transitions in music and career showcase adaptability. Being open to change enables the team to navigate unforeseen challenges.

Step 7: Set High Standards

- **Action:** Establish a culture that strives for excellence.
- **Rationale:** Justin's meticulous approach to his work sets a high standard. Expecting excellence motivates the team to deliver their best.

Step 8: Foster Entrepreneurial Thinking

- **Action:** Encourage entrepreneurial thinking within the team.
- **Rationale:** Justin's foray into entrepreneurship demonstrates a holistic approach. Instilling entrepreneurial thinking sparks creativity and innovation.

Step 9: Celebrate Success and Learn from Failure

- **Action:** Acknowledge achievements and learn from setbacks.
- **Rationale:** Justin's career had highs and lows. Celebrating success boosts morale while learning from failures ensures continuous improvement.

Step 10: Sustain Long-Term Commitment

- **Action:** Foster a long-term commitment to the project.
- **Rationale:** Justin's enduring success is built on commitment. Encourage the team to stay dedicated, knowing that success often comes with sustained effort.

By incorporating these steps inspired by Justin Timberlake's approach, project managers can foster a dynamic, collaborative, and innovative environment that leads to project success.

Here are step-by-step exercises inspired by Justin Timberlake's work ethic and collaborative approach to project management:

Exercise 1: Vision Setting Workshop

1. **Action:** Gather the project team for a vision-setting workshop.
2. **Rationale:** Justin Timberlake's success begins with a clear vision. This exercise helps align team members on project goals and outcomes.

Exercise 2: Skill Diversification Challenge

1. **Action:** Encourage team members to explore a skill outside their expertise.
2. **Rationale:** Justin's multifaceted skills contribute to his success. This exercise promotes cross-functional skills within the team.

Exercise 3: Open Communication Simulation

1. **Action:** Conduct a communication simulation where team members share ideas openly.
2. **Rationale:** Justin's collaborations thrive on communication. This exercise enhances the team's ability to express ideas transparently.

Exercise 4: Creative Exploration Session

1. **Action:** Allocate time for a creative exploration session.

2. **Rationale:** Justin's career is marked by innovation. This exercise fosters a culture of creative thinking and problem-solving.

Exercise 5: Cross-Functional Collaboration Challenge

1. **Action:** Task different departments or teams to collaborate on a specific project.
2. **Rationale:** Justin's collaborations transcend genres. This exercise promotes cross-functional collaboration from diverse perspectives.

Exercise 6: Adaptability Simulation

1. **Action:** Create a scenario requiring the team to adapt quickly.
2. **Rationale:** Justin's transitions showcase adaptability. This exercise hones the team's ability to navigate unforeseen challenges.

Exercise 7: Excellence Recognition Program

1. **Action:** Establish a program to recognize and celebrate excellence.
2. **Rationale:** Justin's meticulous approach sets a high standard. This exercise motivates the team to strive for excellence.

Exercise 8: Entrepreneurial Thinking Workshop

1. **Action:** Conduct a workshop on entrepreneurial thinking.

2. **Rationale:** Justin's entrepreneurship demonstrates a holistic approach. This exercise sparks creativity and an innovative mindset.

Exercise 9: Success and Failure Reflection Session

1. **Action:** Facilitate a session where the team reflects on project successes and failures.
2. **Rationale:** Justin's career had highs and lows. This exercise encourages learning from setbacks and celebrating achievements.

Exercise 10: Long-Term Commitment Pledge

1. **Action:** Have team members express their commitment to the project.
2. **Rationale:** Justin's enduring success is built on commitment. This exercise fosters a sense of dedication among team members.

These exercises aim to instill Justin Timberlake's work ethic and collaborative principles into the project management process, fostering a dynamic and innovative project environment.

Success isn't a sprint; it's a marathon. Find balance and sustainability with weekly insights:

Chapter 12
Billie Eilish

Her superpower is her willingness to be vulnerable and open about her struggles.

"I've always done whatever I want and always been exactly who I am." —Billie Eilish

In the enchanting city of Los Angeles, a musical prodigy was born in 2001, destined to rewrite the rules of the industry. Billie Eilish, the embodiment of raw emotion and unfiltered authenticity, emerged as a beacon for a generation navigating the complexities of the modern world.

Billie's roots in the entertainment industry run deep. Born into a family of musicians and actors, creativity was ingrained in her DNA. However, her journey was far from conventional. Billie's early years were marked by a deep connection to music, a medium she found solace in, allowing her to express the intricate tapestry of her emotions.

Growing up in a world of artistic influence, Billie began crafting her unique sound. Her haunting melodies and introspective lyrics became a mirror reflecting the fears, struggles, and vulnerabilities that define the human experience. It wasn't just about creating music; it was about laying bare the soul for the world to witness.

Billie's "aha" moment came when she recognized the transformative power of authenticity. In an industry often preoccupied with image, she made a conscious choice to be real. This decision to be unapologetically herself, vulnerabilities and all, became the catalyst for her meteoric rise. It wasn't just about making music; it was about being a voice for the voiceless.

As Billie's star ascended, so did the challenges. The music industry, known for its stringent standards of beauty and conformity, attempted to shape her narrative. Yet, Billie stood defiant. She embraced her uniqueness, challenging societal norms and redefining standards of beauty. In her vulnerability, she found strength.

Billie's impact reached beyond the airwaves. She became a trailblazer in destigmatizing conversations around mental health. Through her music, she addressed the struggles faced by today's youth, sparking a global conversation about the importance of mental well-being. Her openness became a lifeline for those grappling with their own challenges.

In 2020, Billie took another step in her journey with the release of *Billie Eilish: The World's a Little Blurry*. The documentary offered an intimate glimpse into her life, capturing the highs and lows of fame, the creative process, and the toll it can take on mental health. It was a testament to her belief that vulnerability is not a sign of weakness but a source of strength.

Awards and accolades have adorned Billie's career, including multiple Grammy Awards. Yet, her focus remains resolutely on the impact she can make through her music. In 2019, she embarked on the "Where Do We Go?" World Tour, not just as a musical journey but as a safe space for fans to connect, share experiences, and find solace in a community that values authenticity.

Billie Eilish's narrative transcends the realm of music. It is a testament to the transformative power of authenticity, a reminder that true strength lies in embracing one's true self. Her journey, marked by vulnerability, has not only defined her career but has become a guiding light for a generation yearning for genuine connection. In a world often obscured by facades, Billie Eilish stands as an inspiration, proving that true empowerment is found in embracing our most authentic selves.

In the realm of portfolio and project management, the journey to success is as much about the technical methodologies and strategic frameworks as it is about the human element of leadership and resilience. The story of Lisa Geraci-Rigoni, a number one bestselling author and Chief Decluttering Officer of the Organizing Mentors, underscores the pivotal role of embracing vulnerability and openness in navigating the complexities of project management and achieving remarkable success.

Lisa's journey is a testament to the power of vulnerability in the professional sphere. Diagnosed with ADD at 40, she faced numerous personal and professional challenges that many would shy away from discussing openly in a business context. Yet, it was her willingness to confront and share her struggles that transformed her challenges into her greatest strengths. By openly addressing her neurodiversity and how it impacted her life and work, Lisa not only fostered a deeper connection with her audience but also illuminated the path for others dealing with similar issues.

Her story is a beacon for project and portfolio managers, emphasizing the importance of staying focused on goals while being open to new opportunities and adapting strategies as needed. Lisa's resilience and adaptability, her ability to declutter not just physical spaces but also the mental and emotional barriers to success, resonate deeply with the principles of effective project management.

In project and portfolio management, like in Lisa's journey, vulnerability is an asset. It encourages a culture of transparency and trust within teams, fostering an environment where challenges are openly discussed and innovative solutions are welcomed. This openness not only enhances collaboration and creativity but also ensures that projects are approached with a comprehensive understanding of potential risks and opportunities.

Moreover, Lisa's ability to adapt her strategies, learn from her experiences, and continuously seek growth and improvement mirrors the agile methodologies that are pivotal in managing complex projects. Her story exemplifies how personal growth and professional methodologies can intersect, leading to enhanced productivity, motivation, and success.

In a landscape marked by rapid technological advancements and shifting market dynamics, the ability to remain focused yet adaptable, disciplined yet open to new ideas becomes crucial. Lisa Geraci-Rigoni's journey through adversity to success encapsulates the essence of effective project and portfolio management. It highlights the importance of embracing one's vulnerabilities, leveraging them as strengths, and maintaining an open mind to navigate the ever-changing terrain of professional challenges and opportunities.

Thus, her narrative not only inspires but also provides a practical blueprint for project and portfolio managers. It illustrates that the path to achieving professional excellence and delivering successful projects is not just about adhering to methodologies and processes but also about embracing the full spectrum of human experience, including the challenges and vulnerabilities that shape us.

"There is no greater agony than bearing an untold story inside you."
—Maya Angelou

The journey of Billie Eilish, transitioning from a Los Angeles-based musical prodigy to an international icon, underscores a fundamental truth that resonates deeply within the domain of portfolio and project management: the power of vulnerability and authenticity. Her story is a vivid illustration of how embracing one's true self, with all its intricacies and vulnerabilities, can lead to unparalleled success and influence, offering invaluable lessons for project managers and leaders.

In portfolio and project management, the ability to be open about struggles and embrace vulnerability is not merely a personal attribute but a strategic advantage. Billie's candidness about her challenges, her unwavering commitment to authenticity, and her refusal to conform to industry norms have not only shaped her music career but also built a profound connection with her audience. This connection, rooted in shared experiences and understanding, has propelled her to unprecedented heights of success.

Similarly, in the realm of project management, leaders who exhibit vulnerability foster a culture of trust and openness. By sharing their challenges and uncertainties, they demystify the notion of infallibility in leadership, encouraging team members to come forward with their ideas, concerns, and solutions. This open dialogue is crucial for identifying potential risks, exploring innovative solutions, and making informed decisions that drive projects forward.

Moreover, Billie's willingness to discuss mental health openly and her efforts to destigmatize these conversations mirror the importance of addressing well-being within project teams. Just as Billie used her platform to initiate discussions on mental health, project managers must acknowledge the human element of their teams, recognizing that the well-being of team members is integral to the project's success. Creating an environment where individuals feel supported and understood can significantly enhance team cohesion, productivity, and, ultimately, the quality of project outcomes.

Billie Eilish's narrative also highlights the significance of adaptability and open-mindedness in the face of adversity. In project management, challenges and setbacks are inevitable. However, staying focused on the end goal while being open to adapting strategies and exploring new opportunities is essential for overcoming obstacles and achieving success. Billie's career trajectory demonstrates that resilience, coupled with an adaptable approach, can lead to groundbreaking achievements.

Eilish's story is a powerful allegory for the principles of effective portfolio and project management. Her journey emphasizes that vulnerability and authenticity are not weaknesses but strengths that can lead to meaningful connections, innovation, and success. As project managers navigate the complexities of their roles, embracing these qualities can transform challenges into opportunities, fostering a culture of trust, collaboration, and resilience that propels projects to their ultimate success.

"The only way to make sense out of change is to plunge into it, move with it, and join the dance." —Alan Watts

"What happens when people open their hearts? They get better." — Haruki Murakami

Gerald J. Leonard

"Vulnerability is the birthplace of innovation, creativity, and change."
—Brené Brown

"Scars remind us where we've been. They don't have to dictate where we're going." —David Rossi (*Criminal Minds*)

How comfortable am I with expressing vulnerability, and how does it impact my relationships with others?

In what ways can being open about my struggles create deeper connections with the people around me?

How do I balance sharing my struggles with maintaining boundaries and protecting my well-being?

Do I view vulnerability as a strength or a weakness, and how does that perspective influence my actions?

How do I ensure that being open about my challenges contributes to my personal growth rather than keeping me stuck?

What role does vulnerability play in fostering trust and authenticity in my work or personal life?

How can I use my own struggles to inspire others and help them feel less alone?

What fears do I have about being vulnerable, and how do those fears affect my relationships or creative work?

How can being open about my challenges help me overcome them and move forward more effectively?

Am I willing to share my struggles when necessary, and how do I create a safe space for others to do the same?

Incorporating Billie Eilish's principles of authenticity, vulnerability, and connecting with others into project management can foster a positive and collaborative work environment. Here are practical steps inspired by Billie's story:

1. **Embrace Authenticity in Team Communication:**
    - Encourage team members to communicate openly and authentically about their challenges, ideas, and concerns.
    - Create a culture that values diverse perspectives, allowing team members to bring their true selves to the project.
2. **Foster a Safe and Inclusive Space:**
    - Establish an environment where team members feel safe sharing their vulnerabilities without fear of judgment.

- Celebrate diversity and uniqueness within the team, recognizing that varied backgrounds contribute to a richer project experience.

3. **Prioritize Mental Health and Well-Being:**
   - Implement policies that support mental health, such as flexible work hours, mental health days, or access to counseling services.
   - Encourage open conversations about mental well-being, reducing the stigma around discussing mental health in the workplace.

4. **Document the Project Journey:**
   - Create a project journal or documentation that captures the highs and lows of the project, similar to how Billie documented her life in the documentary.
   - Reflect on challenges, successes, and the emotional journey of the project to promote a sense of shared experience among team members.

5. **Facilitate Collaborative Creativity:**
   - Establish collaborative spaces for brainstorming and idea-sharing, where team members can contribute freely and explore innovative solutions.
   - Encourage a culture of experimentation and learning from failures, mirroring Billie's approach to her creative process.

6. **Promote Team Bonding and Connection:**
   - Organize team-building activities that go beyond professional roles, allowing team members to connect on a personal level.
   - Host regular check-ins to discuss both work-related matters and personal experiences, fostering a sense of community.

7. **Value and Recognize Individual Strengths:**
   - Acknowledge and celebrate the unique skills and strengths each team member brings to the project.

- Implement a recognition system that appreciates both professional achievements and personal contributions to team dynamics.
8. **Encourage Open Feedback:**
    - Establish a feedback loop where team members can provide constructive feedback openly and receive it positively.
    - Use feedback sessions to continuously improve team dynamics, project processes, and individual performance.
9. **Create a Collaborative Project Documentation:**
    - Develop a collaborative document or platform where team members can contribute insights, lessons learned, and project highlights.
    - Encourage storytelling within the team, sharing experiences that contribute to a collective narrative.
10. **Lead by Example:**
    - Project leaders should embody the principles of authenticity and vulnerability, demonstrating openness, honesty, and a willingness to learn.
    - Share personal experiences related to project challenges and growth, fostering a culture of transparency and continuous improvement.

Incorporating these steps can help create a project management environment that values authenticity, encourages open communication, and prioritizes the well-being of team members, drawing inspiration from Billie Eilish's journey.

1. **Authenticity Icebreaker:**
    - **Objective:** Build trust and encourage authentic communication.

- **Exercise:** Have each team member share a non-work-related fact about themselves that others may not know. This can be a hobby, a personal achievement, or a fun fact. This exercise sets a tone of openness and connection.
2. **Vulnerability Circle:**
    - **Objective:** Foster a safe space for vulnerability.
    - **Exercise:** In a team meeting, designate time for each member to share a professional challenge they're currently facing. Encourage others to provide supportive feedback or share similar experiences. This exercise promotes empathy and collaboration.
3. **Personal Strengths Workshop:**
    - **Objective:** Recognize and celebrate individual strengths.
    - **Exercise:** Conduct a workshop where team members identify and share their personal strengths. Discuss how these strengths contribute to the team's success. Create a visual representation or document showcasing each member's unique contributions.
4. **Project Journaling:**
    - **Objective:** Document the emotional journey of the project.
    - **Exercise:** Introduce a project journaling system. Encourage team members to regularly write about their experiences, challenges, and successes throughout the project. Periodically, dedicate time in team meetings for reflections and shared insights.
5. **Creative Collaboration Session:**
    - **Objective:** Stimulate collaborative and innovative thinking.
    - **Exercise:** Host a creative brainstorming session where team members freely share ideas without judgment. Use creative prompts unrelated to the

project to encourage a mindset of exploration and open collaboration.
6. **Mental Health Check-ins:**
   - **Objective:** Prioritize mental well-being.
   - **Exercise:** Implement regular mental health check-ins during team meetings. Create a scale (e.g., from 1 to 5) where team members anonymously rate their well-being. Discuss trends and explore ways to support each other's mental health.
7. **Storytelling Workshop:**
   - **Objective:** Encourage team members to share experiences.
   - **Exercise:** Organize a storytelling workshop where team members practice sharing anecdotes related to challenges they've overcome or lessons learned. This exercise helps develop effective communication and builds a sense of shared experience.

Craft a personalized plan for lasting productivity—get weekly tips to stay on track:

Conclusion: Building Your Parthenon of Productivity
Constructing Your Legacy

As we draw the final notes from the symphony of lessons presented in this book, it becomes clear that the principles of focus, reinvention, experimentation, and collaboration are not merely ideals—they are actionable frameworks for creating workplaces that thrive. Like the Parthenon, which has endured for centuries as a masterpiece of form and function, the productivity practices we've explored are designed to stand the test of time. Through the lives and legacies of music's greatest icons, we've uncovered the tools to build our own enduring structures, balancing discipline with creativity, resilience with innovation, and individuality with teamwork.

The Four Pillars of Productivity—Focus and Discipline, Reinvention and Innovation, Experimentation and Resilience, Collaboration and Vulnerability—represent the foundation upon which sustainable success is built. These pillars, like the columns of the Parthenon, are distinct yet interdependent. Each strengthens the others, creating a balanced framework that can support even the most ambitious goals.

Focus and Discipline remind us of the importance of clarity and persistence. Just as Prince meticulously controlled every aspect of his craft, successful individuals and teams must prioritize their goals and

Conclusion: Building Your Parthenon of Productivity

commit to seeing them through. Focus is the lens that sharpens our vision, while discipline is the steady hand that keeps us moving forward. Together, they ensure that we don't simply react to the demands of the day but act with purpose, aligning every effort with our larger objectives.

Reinvention and Innovation teach us that success is not static; it requires constant evolution. David Bowie's ability to adapt and redefine himself serves as a powerful reminder that change is not a threat but an opportunity. In the workplace, innovation isn't about novelty for its own sake—it's about finding better ways to solve problems, deliver value, and stay relevant in a rapidly changing world. Reinvention requires courage, but as Bowie showed us, it is also a source of renewal and longevity.

Experimentation and Resilience encourage us to embrace uncertainty and learn from failure. Jimi Hendrix's groundbreaking guitar techniques and Frank Zappa's fearless genre-blending remind us that progress often requires stepping into the unknown. Experimentation fuels creativity, while resilience ensures that setbacks don't derail our efforts but instead become stepping stones to greater achievements. This pillar is about cultivating a mindset that sees challenges not as obstacles but as opportunities for growth.

Collaboration and Vulnerability emphasize the power of connection. No masterpiece—whether it's the Parthenon or a chart-topping album—is created in isolation. Rihanna's ability to foster collaboration across industries and Billie Eilish's openness about her emotions both highlight the importance of working well with others and being authentic in the process. Collaboration multiplies strengths, while vulnerability builds trust and fosters deeper connections. Together, they create a culture where everyone feels valued and empowered to contribute their best.

But how do we translate these lessons into actionable strategies for the workplace? The answer lies in applying the superpowers of these music icons to our own professional lives. Consider the following practical tools and insights:

Conclusion: Building Your Parthenon of Productivity

- **Focus and Discipline:** Start each day by identifying your top priorities. Use tools like project management software or a simple to-do list to organize tasks and track progress. Break large goals into smaller, manageable steps, and set clear deadlines to maintain momentum. Embrace routines that enhance focus, such as dedicated work blocks free from interruptions, and create a culture of accountability where team members are supported in staying on track.
- **Reinvention and Innovation:** Regularly evaluate your processes and be willing to challenge the status quo. Encourage brainstorming sessions where no idea is off-limits, and create an environment where experimentation is celebrated. Use tools like design thinking to approach problems from new perspectives and invest in professional development to keep your skills and strategies fresh.
- **Experimentation and Resilience:** Build flexibility into your plans, knowing that not every experiment will succeed. Use frameworks like Agile to adapt quickly to changes and iterate on ideas. Foster a culture where failure is seen as a learning opportunity and celebrate the lessons gained from taking risks. Develop resilience by focusing on the long-term vision, even when short-term setbacks occur.
- **Collaboration and Vulnerability:** Use collaboration tools to ensure seamless communication and coordination across teams. Create opportunities for team-building and open dialogue, where individuals feel safe sharing ideas and feedback. Lead by example, show vulnerability when discussing challenges or setbacks, and foster a culture of empathy and mutual support.

When these principles are applied consistently, they create a

Conclusion: Building Your Parthenon of Productivity

workplace that not only delivers results but also inspires and engages everyone involved. Like the Parthenon, which continues to awe and educate centuries after its construction, the legacy of a productive workplace extends far beyond its immediate accomplishments.

The enduring legacy of music and the Parthenon lies in their ability to balance harmony and creativity. Music connects us to emotions, stories, and ideas, while the Parthenon connects us to ideals of beauty, balance, and purpose. Together, they offer a powerful metaphor for what a workplace can become when guided by these same principles.

In your own workplace, find the rhythm that keeps your team in sync. Strive for balance, ensuring that no pillar is neglected, just as no column of the Parthenon can be removed without compromising the whole. Embrace the creativity of a musician, the precision of an architect, and the resilience of an enduring structure.

As you move forward, remember that productivity is not just about getting things done; it's about creating something meaningful and lasting. With the lessons of the Four Pillars and the inspiration of music's greatest icons, you have the tools to build your own masterpiece—a workplace that embodies focus, reinvention, experimentation, and collaboration, standing strong for years to come.

The Parthenon stands as a timeless reminder of what's possible when vision, strategy, and execution come together. Let it inspire you to create your own legacy, one that balances harmony and creativity, discipline and innovation, and individuality and teamwork. In the end, like the Parthenon and the icons who have shaped our world, your work can become a source of inspiration, a testament to what's possible when you bring your best to the task. Now, it's your turn to build.

Conclusion: Building Your Parthenon of Productivity

Thank you for joining me on this journey through *Productivity Smarts*! Your path to mastering productivity doesn't end here—it's just beginning. Stay inspired and informed by subscribing to my free weekly newsletter at https://go.growthstrategiesmastermind.com/newsletter, where I share exclusive strategies and actionable tips.

Plus, don't miss the Productivity Smarts Podcast, where I interview world-class productivity thought leaders, authors, and researchers as we dive deep into their latest books, groundbreaking research, and transformative concepts. Let's continue to grow, learn, and achieve greatness together!

Acknowledgments

A sincere thank you to Les Brown, Jack Canfield, and John Peragine for coaching me to success.

www.ingramcontent.com/pod-product-compliance
Ingram Content Group UK Ltd.
Pitfield, Milton Keynes, MK11 3LW, UK
UKHW020247240426
12048UKWH00027B/1657